# Making Quality Happen

Edited by

## Gayner Eyre

Cover designed by Andy Thomsen

I.S.B.N. 0946581 17 7

Printed in Great Britain by BPC Wheatons Ltd, Exeter

# Preface

The aim of this volume is to provide a rationale, framework and ideas for promoting libraries and literature to young people. It does not pretend to be a handbook of 'how to do promotion' although it is hoped that the practical tips given in the case studies and in Chapter 8 will prove a useful aid.

In these days of economic constraints, movement towards privatisation and Citizens Charters, it is easy for the ideology of serving the needs of actual and potential users to become translated into the expediency of concentrating on the demands of the client group, a parallel but not synonymous concept. It is, however, possible and even desirable to combine the two; in fact they must be combined if we are to "make quality happen" through programmes of public relations and promotion. To do this entails setting valid aims and objectives, targeting audiences, careful planning and evaluation, but also being able to justify and demonstrate cost-effectiveness. These are the issues that are addressed here.

The volume concentrates on promoting public libraries and school libraries but does not attempt to cover school library services, as the particular marketing requirements for promoting such services warrant a separate volume. Although all the case studies are drawn from public libraries, it is hoped that the ideas, methodologies and guidance will be of general interest to any librarian promoting services to children.

Part I provides a rationale and overview. Part II consists of four case studies which are examples of projects which have worked, but both pitfalls and opportunities are highlighted. Part III ends the work with handy hints.

Good luck with any promotions you undertake.

Gayner Eyre
February 1994

# CONTENTS

# PART I

# WHY PROMOTE?

# INTRODUCTION

## PUBLIC RELATIONS, PROMOTION AND LIBRARIES IN CONTEXT

**Gwil Huws and Gayner Eyre**

> Good libraries empower. Using their resources can unfetter our imaginations; disclose hitherto unrealised worlds; promote knowledge; induce pleasure; make us laugh; impart insights; challenge our misconceptions; assuage fears; prick our conscience; inflame our sensibilities; and provide professional refreshment. What we learn from good books and other resources becomes part of us. (1)

'Good Libraries empower.' All good librarians will recognise and concur with the statements made in the opening quotation. However, this empowerment is available only to those with access to and knowledge of all those facilities offered by a good library. Potential users do not start from a level base. Some will have far more advantages than others, resulting from factors such as background, education, literacy and proximity to adequate library facilities. To redress the imbalance it is therefore necessary for any 'good library' to incorporate public relations and promotions' strategies into the infrastructure of the library's policies and practices. It is arguably especially true where children and young people are concerned as access to such facilities may help to create the foundation for a fulfilled life.

Public relations and promotion is a long established part of services to children and young people. Promotion for libraries in general has been seen as increasingly important and in the States (2) this has been refined to the extent of broadcasting jingles on radio and advertisements on television. As a part of service delivery, PR and promotion has also suffered changing fortunes according to current philosophies and circumstances in public and schools library services.

However, before examining in more detail the importance of PR and promotion in the context of public library services to children and school libraries, it may be useful to discuss briefly the purpose of PR and promotion in general, together with any specific problems relating to promoting library and information work. Many definitions of public relations exist and the following by Mildred Knight Laughton gives a reasonable summary:

... a planned, continuous communication effort designed to gain support by developing mutual understanding and co-operation between an organization and its publics. (3)

To develop 'mutual understanding and co-operation' with potential customers, organizations will use promotional and PR techniques: a) to identify the range of 'products' available, b) to make the potential customer aware of these 'products', c) to introduce prospective customers to representatives of the organisation, d) to persuade potential customers of the benefits of 'buying' or using those products.

Effective communication between organisations and their potential customers is critical to all PR and promotional activity. There are various communication channels open to an organisation which will help improve the public's awareness of a product or stimulate potential customers to buy or use its products. One could communicate a message;

—personally e.g. face to face encounter
—environmentally e.g. decor or displays
—using media presentation both in-house e.g. printed leaflets or videos and through the wider media e.g. local radio
—through activities e.g. demonstrations, talks and other events.

Decisions regarding the appropriate communication channel to use in a particular situation would depend on factors such as opportunity, the target audience and the resources available.

When we turn our attention to PR and promotion in the field of libraries there are certain problems created by the nebulous quality of the 'product', i.e. information and services. Also there are difficulties in placing a value on this 'product' because it is generally held that access to information is one of the pre-conditions of a truly democratic society and there is a long tradition that information should be available free of charge through the library service. Other difficulties facing those who wish to promote library and information services within an organisation include a low awareness of customer wants and needs and the problem of relating the value of its products and services to the mission and goals of that organisation.

A knowledge and understanding of what is being promoted and an enthusiasm for it, underpins all successful PR and promotion. The largest problem confronting those who wish to promote the image and the products of library and information services, however, is the realisation that most of the public are uncertain of the role which librarians play in society today. This is hardly surprising given that the profession itself is undergoing a certain amount of self-examination as evidenced by reactions to the Comedia report (4), and the institution of the DFE and LISC working parties set up to examine public library provision and library services to children and schools respectively. This re-examination is particularly pertinent when set against the background of recent legislation.

The 1990's will be a critical phase in the history of the public library service. In addition to social and technological developments, libraries will face major political changes ... It is undoubtedly true that the public library

7

service will have to galvanise itself into action if it is to avoid being smothered by the embrace of those who wish to privatise it. (5)

The Local Government and Housing Act (1988) (6) began the thrust towards privatisation by giving public libraries the option to charge for all but the most basic services. This movement has gained momentum through Compulsory Competetive Tendering (CCT) amongst other things, opening the door for whole sections of the public library service to be run on a private basis. The Education Reform Act and subsequent related legislation has also had a devastating effect both on the way schools operate and on the provision of local government services to those schools. Many school library services are now operating as a stand-alone business and their very existence depends on convincing schools to 'buy-back' the service.

A recently published examination of some of these issues proposes three marketing strategies which should be adopted to meet the challenge of improving the perception of the library profession:

1 Clarify the nature of our products and services to create a unique selling proposition that can be more easily assimilated by our customers, real and potential;
2 Offer everyone a lifetime library and information entitlement, a right to our highest quality of service, through improved diffusion of our best practice across all organizational sectors;
3 improve the internal harmony of our profession to create a sharper and more unified focus on common issues and a common sense of mission and purpose to project to those outside. (7)

PR and promotion has always been important, but in the light of recent changes it takes on a new aspect and a new urgency. Ironically, in the accompanying squeeze on public sector finance, funding for effective PR and promotion is often seen as a low priority and an easy target for cuts. It has therefore become essential that the value and role of libraries of all kinds are communicated effectively to the potential users, those who have control of budgets and politicians at all levels.

**References**
1. Library Association: Learning Resources in Schools. Library Association Guidelines for School Libraries. LA, 1992, p.5.
2. R. Usherwood: The visible library: practical public relations for public librarians. London: LA, 1981.
3. M. K. Laughlin & E. H. Latrobe: Public relations for school library media centers. Englewood (Colarado): Libraries Unlimited, 1990, p.1.
4. Borrowed time? the future of public libraries in the U.K. Gloucestershire: Comedia, 1993.
5. M. Fisher, M. P. IN I. King: Promote! The handbook of public library promotions. Leicester: Public Libraries Group of the Library Association, 1989. pp. ii–iii.
6. Local Government and Housing Act 1988. London: H.M.S.O., 1988.
7. A. Irving: Marketing the information profession to the information society. London: Library Association, 1990. (Viewpointsin Lis; 7) p. ix.

# CHAPTER 1

## PROMOTING PUBLIC LIBRARIES AND LITERATURE FOR YOUNG PEOPLE

Gayner Eyre

### Rationale

The Library Association Guidelines on Public library services to children and young people (1) states

> Promotion is a vital and integral part of service delivery and is not something to be added on. Promotional strategies should, therefore, be built into service development at the planning stage ...

The LA Guidelines provide valuable support to librarians, particularly in public libraries, but also in school libraries and any others which serve children or those working with them. Support is crucial at the present time when there are many upheavals in the public sector resulting from budget constraints and government legislation. Senior managers and local politicians, by necessity, are now being forced to streamline services, to justify services if not to make substantial cuts. Promotional activities are often regarded as a frill, something 'added on' and consequently an easy target for cuts. This means that not only is it desirable but absolutely vital to think about why we are undertaking promotion and to be able to justify this to those who have budgetary and decision-making powers.

To some extent the justification of promotion will depend on the aims and objectives of the organisation or authority. In some authorities it will be easier than in others; for example a library service may have an overall objective of

'helping the individual to achieve his/her rights within a democratic society".

To meet this objective it is important to make sure that every individual from a very young age, or his/her carer knows

a) that the library exists
b) what it can offer
c) how to gain access to the service points
d) how to exploit facilities and information sources

Whatever the philosophy of the parent body, promotional activities must be set within the context of that philosophy to succeed and to be relevant.

But there are reasons for promoting other than helping an organisation to achieve its goal. These reasons are perhaps more important. The service philosophy behind the LA Guidelines begins with the individual child and the world within which today's children live. Within this context his/her needs are determined and only then translated into terms of what a library or library service has to offer. Successful PR and promotion begins with understanding the world and needs of children, a belief in the valuable part that library resources can play in this, and a knowledge of the services and materials available. Only then is it possible to work out the strategies to make services and resources as accessible as possible to every child.

The LA guidelines (2) exemplify some ways in which children can benefit from libraries, and what libraries have to offer:-

From library materials:-

* Enjoyment: of story experience, of language, of associated art etc.
* Knowledge of the wider world.
* Understanding of other people: behaviour, culture, situations.
* self-knowledge.
* Information.
* Confidence in the acquisition of vocabulary, speech and language skills [and support for reading skills].
* Shared experiences between adult and child.
* Support for formal and informal education.

From libraries

* Assistance and Guidance ...
* Access to materials ... [and literature]
* Access to service at a choice of times and places
* Access ... to a greater library network
* A neutral ground ... for independent and unhindered discovery
* A place to learn and practice information skills ...

In summary, library services to children and young people may:

provide support for a child's emotional, intellectual and educational development
provide access to society and culture
help towards preparing a child for a literate society

Libraries provide for children's leisure, educational, emotional and intellectual needs. They provide a "uniquely objective source of information for young people, enabling them to discover and use the power of access that information skills can bring in the society of today and tomorrow". (3)

The above pointers demonstrate the value of libraries, materials and library services to young people. The fact that all these exist and are available is of little use, however, to the individual who is unaware of them. Again from the LA Guidelines; (4)

1. Surveys have shown that most habitual adult library users were library users as children.
2. Children from all backgrounds and cultures have an equal right of access to all the benefits listed above.
3. Every child is a potential user and should be reached in some way.
4. Not all children and young people are fortunate enough to have parents or carers who will introduce them to literature, libraries and information sources.
5. Knowledge is power. Access to that knowledge can provide a foundation-stone for life. Access can only be achieved if that which is available is known.
6. Children are at the beginning of life and have the right to know what is available to them, either directly or through the adults that care for them whether parent or teacher.

Put within the context of these statements, it becomes clear that reaching out through promotion and public relations is essential to any quality library service for children.

Having clarified the philosophies and justifications behind promoting library services, the next step is to examine the various elements which may give the impetus for promotion and to look at the target groups at whom any promotion is aimed.

## Promoting children's literature and libraries in the Public Library

Any promotional activities should have clear, stated objectives. There should be a defined purpose for every activity, leaflet, or community visit. At this point therefore, decisions must be made on what is being promoted, why it is being promoted and to whom.

Below are some suggested occasions when some form of promotion is called for.

To increase awareness of the library in general, to let the public (or others) know it is there.
To advertise a new service or service-point.
To promote services to special client groups, e.g. under fives, dyslexic children, teenagers.
To exploit literature, whether fiction and non-fiction.
To encourage reading.
To increase awareness of support to both formal and informal education.
To introduce children and adults to the library and also to its facilities and stock.
To introduce and provide instruction in the use of library materials.
To promote the library as a community facility, a meeting place or information point, and to act as an outlet for promoting community activities.
To raise awareness of current or topical issues.
To act as a cultural centre for the promotion of the arts.
To forge links with others whose objectives complement those of the library.

## Who

In the area of children's services there are a vareity of potential target groups. It is useful when considering promotion to aim this at a defined sector of the community.

This may be a general catch-all, embracing children across a number of age range for example, or may be aimed at specific groups. Any decision to this effect shoul be made explicit at the planning stage. Target groups may be as follows:

1. Children of all ages and abilities and from a wide range of cultural backgrounds (The individual 'groups' such as 'under fives' may be targeted separately).
2. Parents and carers, particularly for the preschool age group.
3. Teachers.
4. Staff including management.
5. The profession.
6. Local officials e.g. councillors.
7. Education officials and school governors.

Margaret Marshall in her **An introduction to the world of children's books** (5 provides an exhaustive listing of possible target groups. 'Each of these offer differen promotional opportunities which need to be thought through.'

## Where

Another decision also has to be made at the planning stage and that is where th promotional activity should take place. This will again be determined by the targe audience and the reason for promotion.

### 1. In the library

The first and most obvious place for promotional activities to take place is withi the library itself whether it be a school library or a public library services point This is particularly important for introductions to the library, breaking dow barriers, encouraging children over the threshold and getting them used to usin the library.

The library building and environment, the quality and state of stock, access to tha stock and other services, the attitude of the staff and the quality of service receive are all potent factors in determining whether or not children and adults will use th library. They are therefore issues which play a large part in PR and promotion. T use marketing jargon there is absolutely no point in publicising if the product i not right.

To take these issues singly, the building should be the first consideration. Ideall the children's library will be well situated, giving maximum accessibility to al potential users including very young children, parents with prams, children wit disabilities and any other individual with possible mobility problems. This woul suggest a ground floor location wherever possible. Large windows with attractiv displays or alternatively where children can be seen reading or working will als encourage use. In the case of a school library the environment should be conduciv to the function of the library, are there areas where pupil's can work quietly fo example? However, the actual building and its layout are often things that ar beyond the control of the librarian unless involved in planning of a new library But there are many things that can be done to ensure that the environment i welcoming and attractive to young people; appropriate furnishings, bright colours attractive displays and exhibitions including children's own work, mobiles, posters toys, plants. Many children's libraries now have 'feature furniture' as a focal poin such as shelving in the shape of cars, trains or dragons on which children can play. Newcastle pioneered the idea of a 'theme library' when they designed the interior as a street, with alley ways between the bookshelves. Waterthorpe library in Sheffield has a story booth designed as a castle. Many publishers and suppliers now produce posters and mobiles, stickers and dump bins advertising books and authors, many available free of charge. These may be used to brighten up the library and are particularly useful if money is short.

The LA Guidelines say that to children 'visual impact is all important' (6). This is also verified by comments from educationalists advising on support for the National Curriculum. The English curriculum particularly calls for visual and literary stimulus in a child's surrounding. Examples given are posters, guiding, ephemera, displays and the written work of other children. The library is seen as a place which facilitates such display.

The quality and state of the stock speaks for itself. If there is nothing there of interest to a child, he/she is not encouraged to return. The more often a child is disappointed when seeking a specific item or materials of a given topic, the less likely they are to return. Similarly, if stock is falling to pieces it is unlikely to be very attractive. In days of cut-backs this is something which should be given careful thought. The same applies to adults such as parents wanting to use a parent's information collection, teachers using the school library service or library within school.

Gaining access to the library and its materials and services is very important for all. Firstly, is the library signposted, can it be found without too much trouble? Is there access for children and adults with disabilities? Once inside the library how easy is it for children to gain access to materials and information? It is very important to have adequate guiding, attractive and accessible arrangement of materials, for example, kinderboxes for picture books, face-on display for paperbacks and areas of stock highlighted in displays. Although it is now recognised by educational psychologists that all individual children have special needs, those for whom English is a second language, those with reading difficulties, aural or visual impairment or dyslexia amongst others may have particular problems when using the library. In good systems such as Birmingham, much thought has gone into making library facilities accessible to these groups. Although their needs are disparate quite often one solution may suffice, for example most groups (except children who have visual problems) require very clear, simple guiding with unambiguous visual symbols. In addition the layout of the library should be logical, material shelved at the right height for the age group and any indexes and catalogues should be easy enough to use for the appropriate age-group. This is important in any library but particularly so for children who may be easily daunted by not being able to find what they require on their own.

It is important that the attitude of the staff of the library is positive. This applies not only to the staff specifically responsible for children's services, but for all those who may come into contact with young people and relevant adults. How children are treated is an important consideration. Are staff welcoming and helpful? Are young people treated as of equal importance to adults? Ultimately, are they treated in a manner which would encourage them to return? (apply this to teenagers, a group which often cause attitude problems amongst staff.) Customer care is one of the major concerns of most library services and is seen as being an important determinant in the image of the library. This philosophy should extend to children's services.

Of course, adults or children must be able to obtain the services they want and need. Do librarians know what the needs are? This is something that many school library services are now having to question, and to survive many are undertaking surveys to ascertain the services most valued by teachers. In many authorities there are some surprises!

The library in question may not be a static service point but a vehicle, a book bus or mobile library for example. The LA Guidelines (7) advocate a bright, colourful exterior design to enhance their appeal to children. Inside the same principles apply as to a fixed service-point. Vehicles have the advantage of mobility and can be used in major events or to target client groups not near library buildings.

## 2. In the community
The meaning of community in this section is basically the population served by a particular library, be it a school, branch or central children's library. Outreach (considered by some an outdated term now and by others as the precursor to promotion) is exactly what it says, reaching out to that community. There is growing recognition that 'the library' is not a building. It may be based within a building but services, facilities and functions extend beyond these confines and will necessitate undertaking promotional activities in the wider community. Ivan King argues that the original intention of outreach was to recruit users but that this concept is now accepted as having little validity by the library profession, and has been transplanted by the promotion of reading and promoting the library as a community resource for leisure and information. (8)

One of the functions of outreach may be to extend provision of library services and materials into various centres and establishments within the community. Particular client groups have forced librarians to re-think the parameters of the library service. To give an example, it is widely accepted that library use falls when children reach mid-teens so some librarians maintained that if teenagers will not go to the library, the library should be taken to them. Nottinghamshire set up an extensive programme of deposit collections in youth centres in the 1970's and early 80's although financial constraints are now forcing library services to re-think such strategies.

The purpose of promoting in the community may be to target traditional non-users of library services and resources. An example may be pre-school children in an inner city area where parents do not see the library as a priority.

Promotion of books and reading may also take place in the community:

* storytelling in parks.
* taking a bookbus to areas not served by a library, particularly useful in rural areas.
* handing out booklists and leaflets in busy places such as Sainsbury's or the local post office.

* books talks in schools, in assembly, in class, at parents evenings or open days.

Promotion may take place in the community when trying to encourage new library members. Schools and nurseries provide a captive audience conveniently brought together. Several authorities, believing in the 'catching them young' theory now target new and expectant mothers in maternity hospitals with book displays, leaflets and even enrolment forms in 'new mothers' packs'. When new service points are opened, often temporary enrolment desks are set up in focal points for the community such as shopping precincts or community buildings.

Outreach activities may also be applied to a school library where the school is the immediate community. Making contacts in the staff room, attending head of department meetings, parents evenings, visiting feeder schools are all elements of outreach.

The important point is that working out in the community ensures that non-users of the library are targeted and they are arguably more important in terms of promotional activities than those children and adults who use the library service as a matter of course.

The calendar is often used as an impetus for promotional activities so that festivals and holidays will form the content and methodology of promotion. Examples of such would be Christmas, Easter, Eid, Diwali or Chinese New Year. Using a multicultural calendar may ensure that all sectors of the community are considered. The selection of a theme will of course be dictated by the make-up of the particular community in question.

It is worth nothing here that all this presupposes a knowledge of both the local and wider community, an essential prerequisite for any good quality service to children.

### 3. In the wider community
The wider community is taken here to mean the community of a library authority rather than one localised service point. Usually this is used for major events which may be city or county-wide or, as in the case of Bookweek in Northern Ireland, country-wide. Of course events may be smaller than this taking in parts of authorities which are areas greater than the localised community. For major initiatives, events and activities may literally be held anywhere. Usually key factors are adequate space and reaching as wide an audience as possible. The Crucible Theatre in Sheffield hosted many bookfairs, Trafford used a large sports hall for a major event (which was televised by Blue Peter). Other locations may be other Council buildings, shops (storyhours in Debenhams?—it has been done), shopping precincts, bandstands. Again the location may not be stationary. Hertfordshire's famous storyboat called off at stops along the river and National Bookweek organisers have used a train which stopped to tell stories at various stations.

Imagination is a great asset when planning such events, but ideas need to be backed up with contacts and practicality, and it must be remembered when dealing with children, particularly some groups such as the very young or those with disabilities, safety is a key consideration.

There are usually two stages to promotion:

1. Putting on a promotional event or activity, or producing a booklist, magazine etc.
2. Publicising that event.

The inference is that even if an event is to be held in the library it may be necessary to get out into the community (or to use press channels which will be dealt with later) to publicise this. The extent to which this is done will vary tremendously according to the population served. A librarian in an inner-city library will usually have to work far harder at encouraging attendance that will a librarian serving a population mainly consisting of professional people where it may be sufficient just to put a poster in the library. (One busy library in Sheffield had a waiting list for a regular under fives' session. This was so long that children had often started school by the time their name came to the top of the list.)

In conclusion, despite economic constraints promotion and PR should ideally be proactive. This means going out into the community to promote libraries and literature rather than waiting for members of the community to come through the door.

## How
Methods of promotion are many and various. The target audience, the reason for promoting and the resources available will dictate the nature of the activity. To give an example: If a new service point has opened and there has been a decision to advertise the fact to the local community more 'gimmicky' tactics may be employed e.g. the use of children's entertainers or a party. The objective here is to attract the community through the doors and to break down any barriers between the staff and the community. On the other hand, if the objective is to promote an area of stock, for example poetry, then the approach would be completley different and activities may include poetry reading, a poetry workshop run by a local poet, or the use of drama to focus on one or two specific poems. Activities may fulfil several functions, but the key point is that the methodology should fulfil the objectives.

There is not enough space within this chapter to list all the possibilities for promotion. It is recognised that in these times of financial constraints some of these activities may appear unrealistic. No apology is made for this as the aim here is to spark imagination and offer a source of inspiration.

PR and promotion can be categorised under general headings, some of which are listed below.

1. Printed materials
2. Promotional talks
3. User education
4. Displays and exhibitions
5. Events and activities
6. Using the media
7. Giveaways or sale items

(Working with others could be included here but is included as a separate section as it may have a multi-purpose function.)

## 1. Printed materials

Printed materials may have various purposes and forms, but basically they are produced to convey information or to promote the library and its facilities. Examples are;

1. posters, fliers and leaflets.
2. booklists.
3. magazines.
4. press releases.
5. stickers etc.

Posters and leaflets may be used to advertise anything from new opening hours and details on service points to major events. They may highlight authors, books or awards such as Carnegie/Kate Greenaway Medals. Posters may be available from a number of organisations such as publishers but many will be provided in-house. Booklists speak for themselves. The LA Guidelines say that for printed materials

> Careful thought must be given to issues such as format, appropriate language, illustrations, layout, housestyle, quantity, distribution and funding . . . Visual impact and size of print are particularly important features. (9)

As with any promotional material printed items should have a clear purpose and a target audience. Amongst many others, Nottinghamshire and Hampshire provide a range of very attractive leaflets outlining aspects of service and booklists for varying age groups. These are well produced on glossy paper, attractively designed and illustrated usually in full colour.

Magazines have risen and fallen in popularity. They may contain booknews, articles on authors and may have a wider scope. Rotherham's Freewheeler, the magazine of the mobile library service also contains jokes, recipes, interesting facts and other items related to stock, as well as details of library stopping points and times, forthcoming events and other such items. The lightheartedness of items, drawn from the stock of the mobile service ensure that readers will be tempted to pick it up, and so come across some of the more serious messages. Magazines may also include the work of young people, perhaps stories, poems, reviews. This is a popular activity with those serving teenagers. Producing glossy, attractive magazines can however be a costly business and is an area for which it is probably worth investigating sponsorship.

Press releases are usually issued when there is anything of note which requires a wide audience.

Stickers may also be classed with giveaways or items for sale. As with any printed material they may publicise the library, series of books, or reading clubs amongst other items. Often libraries produce their own, or they can be obtained from publishers, suppliers and often the organisers of National events. They may be given away for activities, in the streets during major events or after reading so many books in a reading club and they always seem popular with children.

## 2. Promotional Talks

Promotional talks are a very cost-effective way of promoting libraries and stock to a large number of people. They can be used to promote particular areas of stock or literature for a specific age group, and offer the opportunity for immediate feedback.

Such talks may be to children or to parents, teachers, nursery staff. Often they take place in schools or playgroups, but may also occur in clinics, hospitals or on the radio.

## 3. User Education

User education may take place on a formal or informal basis. It may be giving a primary school class a brief introduction to the library or it may be part of an intensive information skills programme within a school.

Some public library systems have a very developed formal programme of 'library instruction'. These usually include exercises and instruction on using catalogues, basics such as alphabetical order and information retrieval. Students may be introduced to using a variety of information sources e.g. microfiche, newspapers, archives materials and larger reference works, and will be shown how to access the information within those sources.

At a more advanced level IS training may be targeted to a specific subject with an introduction to reference materials within that subject, including bibliographics, indexes, abstracts and literature guides within that subject. An introduction to CD ROM and computerised databases may be included alone with some basic research skills.

## 4. Displays and exhibitions

Displays and exhibitions may be mounted within the library or erected by librarians in schools, art centres, or other such venues. Whatever their form they are promoting the library and its resources.

Displays can be used to promote stock and specific issues concerning stock e.g. National Curriculum, Carnegie and Kate Greenaway winners. They may tie in with the initiative of another organisation e.g. a school's parents evening, a museum's archaeology display. Conversely the facilities of others may be used to enhance displays within the library e.g. natural history artefacts from the museum, literature or posters from friends of the Earth or 'Greenpeace' to complement a display on the environment. (There is great scope for flair and inventiveness here—I have seen huge model ships and aeroplanes being used).

The library may display and exhibit the work of other agencies e.g. pupils' work from local schools, a display by a local community group. Some authorities e.g. Birmingham are now displaying literary works of the local community such as stories, poems and reviews. Displays may be on wider issues e.g. a local health authority display about caring for teeth, the problems connected with German measles, or there may be a crime-prevention display by the local police. Other council departments may wish to use library outlets for their own publicity, for example, children's art exhibitions.

18

## 4. Events and Activities

"Traditionally events and activities have been a particularly significant element in library work with children" (LA Guidelines). (10) They may have many functions some of which may be to

1. Promote and exploit stock.
2. promote reading.
3. promote and create a positive image of the library and its services.
4. support formal and informal education.
5. target a specific client group.
6. promote culture.
7. provide a community function.

The general principles of promotion apply here. The kind of activity will be determined by the rationale behind the activity.

Again because of the diversity of events it is impossible to provide an exhaustive list but below are some examples of relevant events and activities.

The objective of large-scale events may be two-fold i.e. to promote both the library services and literature for children. These may be held as part of National events such as Children's Bookweek, part of local events such as literary or cultural festivals, or may be an initiative by the library to promote facilities for a particular age-group such as under fives' or a particular issue such as Environment Week. Large scale events often encompass a programme of many promotional techniques e.g. the 1989 Bookweek in Sheffield comprised over 100 events and included radio broadcasts, displays, staff in costume, talks, exhibitions, stickers and giveaways and workshops.

Usually it is possible and desirable to use well-known authors and celebrities to attract larger crowds. The bookfair held at the end of the week mentioned included sessions by Floella Benjamin and Michael Palin who managed to draw crowds of 5–6000. The previous day hosted a series of authors' workshops, held for school classes, and among the authors were Andrew Davies (author of Marmalade Atkins books), Andrew Taylor (author of the Coal House) and the poet, Wes Magee. Derbyshire have at various times had John Noakes (ex Blue Peter) and Rolf Harris. It is, of course, essential to investigate and make the appropriate provision for fees.

Large scale events are characterised by having a central theme and central co-ordination. Because they are so large and held over a reasonably long period they tend to attract far more media coverage which is an added advantage when trying to appeal to large numbers of people.

Many of the activities making up a large event would be used for individual activities. To keep costs to a reasonable level local authors and celebrities may be used and also local talent, for example a local band for teenagers. Usually routine and local activities are on a much more modest scale.

It may be useful at this stage to differentiate between the kinds of activities used for differing purposes and to give one or two examples.

a) To advertise a new service or library service-point the following activities may be used:

* using entertainers—magicians, community circuses, puppet shows, pantomimes by a local theatre group, etc.
* fancy dress parties.
* putting on a fair with games e.g. quoits, hoopla etc.

b) Exploiting literature may be different for fiction and non-fiction.

To promote fiction the following techniques may be used:

* drama either workshops or through local theatre groups.
* puppets (often used for multicultural tales e.g. Anansi stories).
* flannelgraphs (these are useful in encouraging children to participate).
* storytelling.
* author visits.
* prose and poetry readings by librarians, authors or local actors.
* film and video showings.

There is a growing trend for activities to be participative and to encourage children to be creative. Ideas for this are:

* writers in residence schemes e.g. Calderdale had Berlie Doherty for two years.
* poetry workshops.
* facilities and display space for children's own review and writing.

Promotion of non-fiction may be even more varied. Often activities will be supported by displays of books, materials and artefacts, posters and AV materials etc. Some examples are as follows:

* treasure trails and quizzes where children must use library materials to answer questions e.g. Norfolk's Treasure Island scheme. Sometimes but not always there are prizes awarded for completion.
* activities to promote specific sections of stock e.g. craft activities, sports or computer evenings.
* demonstrations by local groups e.g. make-up or fashion for teenagers, fire engines and police dogs for younger children.
* talks by local people e.g. on topical issues say a talk by the drugs squad, or on natural history by the local Natural History Society (In Sheffield there was a woman who kept exotic pets—snakes, large spiders etc. and a man who looked after owls. Both were prepared to talk to children).

It is worth noting here that although some expect a fee, many local groups are often only too pleased to be able to promote their services and will offer talks free of charge, an important consideration for librarians on limited budgets.

c) Many activities listed above may be used to support reading. Reading may additionally be promoted through reading clubs, schemes or reading trees. Many library systems have their own version of these, but basically a child will be given a range of books to read. Having read so many, and perhaps having answered questions on them he/she may receive a badge, or a star, or a leaf to put on his/her reading tree. Each level of achievement is rewarded in such a way as to enable a child to see what progress has been made.

d) Supporting formal and informal education.

User Education which has already been discussed is a key method of supporting both formal and informal education. It may be tied into the curriulum whether offered through the school or public library but it has the added benefit of fostering self-help and therefore provides a grounding for discovery in all areas.

Some other ways of supporting formal education are:

* class visits (from school to library)
* talks in school
* homework sessions

Most of the methods described in this section will be used to support informal education

e) Targeting a specific group

This has been mentioned here as in the days of cut-backs priorities must be set. It is felt by many authorities that promotion should target client groups who do not traditionally use the library service or who are unaware of the service. Two groups may be teenagers and under fives. Although the methods used for promotion will be the same as general promotion it is obvious that they must be geared to the interest of the targeted group. e.g. events for teenagers may be:

* music evenings
* computer workshops
* make-up demonstrations
* talks by the drugs squad etc.

Under fives activities may be

* messy play sessions
* teddy bear's picnics
* storytime.

f) Promoting Culture.

There is growing agreement that libraries are cultural centres. Just as art galleries are there to promote art, libraries should promote literature including poetry, prose, drama. There is also a tendency to encourage literature which is of the community itself, not just from mainstream publishers. Often the function of writers in residence is to vet manuscripts of local people and to hold writing workshops, for children as well as adults. Many of the activities are similar to those used to promote stock.

It may not only be literature, but also visual arts that are promoted by libraries. Illustrators' workshops and demonstrations are an example. Jan Pienkowski, illustrator of a number of pop-up books including Haunted House (11) and Dinner Time (12) involves children in painting massive murals and friezes. Art departments may collaborate and provide art displays.

Music may be promoted through listening groups, local bands or musical games. One librarian I knew played classical music from commercials. Teenagers had to guess the commercial and then they were introduced to each piece in its original form.

Libraries may be cultural centres in the true sense of the word highlighting local culture e.g. local history talks or quizzes, or may highlight the cultures of children representing the various groups within the community e.g. Caribbean cookery evenings, Eid parties, celebrations for Chinese New Year. There are several storytelling groups working nationwide who use song, dance and story from a culture to give an insight to that culture.

g) Providing a community function.

Libraries whether public or schools often have an advantage over other services such as museums or arts in that they are an integral part of the community, or have a network of services reaching several communities.

Libraries may fulfil a community function in a number of ways. The multicultural activities outlined above may perform the function of bringing various elements within a community together or to create a greater understanding of the various cultures within a community.

A library may fulfil a community function by making space and buildings available, for example the local playgroup may meet there. It may be through acting as an outlet for services offered by others e.g. an outlet for a local toy library. Alternatively the children's librarian may offer activities such as storytelling workshops for parents.

### 6. Using the media
Using the media has obvious advantages for public relations and promotion as it is possible to get a message across to a wider audience. One of the most common uses of media is through local radio and newspapers. It is useful to have contacts here and these are obviously built up by usage. There are several ways the various media can be used.

* Press releases on events, new services etc. to newsdesks may be picked up as a news item, and if sent well enough in advance may be picked up as a feature for an article, or the radio may send a radio car round to an event.
* Details of times, places and contents of events may be included in the diaries of the medium.
* Librarians may be invited onto radio programmes to talk about books or issues. This is usually at times such as Christmas to highlight 'good buys', or when somethings controversial is happening such as banning racist/sexist material (remember Noddy books? and Dr. Dolittle?)

Librarians may be proactive and approach the radio station which may lead to a regular slot. Staff of Bradford Libraries at one time had a regular book programme on Radio Aire. Competitions, quizzes or regular reviews may be run through the children's page or section of the local newspaper.

Children, character costumes, and some events present wonderful photo opportunities which may attract the press and result in coverage. (The librarian may have a photo taken and send it to the paper).

Television or national coverage is much harder to obtain and will need either a big name, controversial focus or something very special. Calderdale for one of its Bookweek events received television coverage on one of the Saturday morning children's programmes.

It is often advisable when planning big events to involve media contacts from the planning stage. Media coverage only works if thought, planning and work has gone into achieving it.

### 7. Giveaways and sale items
Usually these are given away as part of or after an event. The 'goody bag' is becoming almost a compulsory feature of major events (in addition to generating income in some cases). Providing items containing the library logo, booklists or the name of an event gives something for children to take away.

Not only is this popular it also means that they have a reminder with them. Giveaways may take the form of balloons, pencils, erasers, bookmarks, badges, lapel stickers, carrier bags. Sale items may include pens, mugs, T shirts, key-rings— Sutton supply umbrellas!

### Working with others
Working with others in promotion is often of mutual benefit to libraries and to other agencies and individuals. Reasons may be

1. to forge links with groups and organisations whose objectives complement those of the library and to promote common aims.
2. to maximise resources—money, human resources, space, communication channels etc.
3. to take advantage of grants, awards and sponsorship in whatever form.
4. There is often a secondary advantage and that is it opens up channels of communication and can provide valuable feedback on stock and services and provide a useful network of contacts.

Such a co-operation may take place on:

1. a local basis
2. an authority-wide basis
3. a national basis.

Within the local community librarians may wish to work with such groups as schools, playgroups, mother and toddler groups and youth centres, either to raise the profile of the library with these groups or to provide joint ventures such as activities—book fairs, bookweeks in schools, open days. Groups may be invited to support a library initiative or library staff may take advantage of promotion opportunities opened by events held by others, in providing talks, displays or other support. Paying the fees and expenses of authors or theatre groups may be diluted by 'sharing'. It may be that the library joins in local community events such as pageants and festivals.

The library may jointly produce publications such as a magazine for teenagers with the local youth centre. If the library provides a newsletter community groups may be asked to contribute and vice-versa. Many under fives groups produce local newsletters and many communities produce publications. They are often very grateful for contributions and offer a tremendous opportunity for free publicity in the form of articles, annotated booklists, details of library services etc.

It is important that library staff do work with others in the community when planning events and activities:

1. to maximise help and advice
2. so that activities do not clash (e.g. running a session for teenagers when there is a disco at the local school)
3. so that the events of various organisations may be dove-tailed. An example is that local authorities often run Summer playschemes. Funding for this may be devolved to several departments. Getting together can mean sharing buildings, facilities, publicity and will facilitate a co-ordinated plan.

On a wider basis the central offices or umbrella organisations of many of the groups mentioned are useful when co-ordinating large scale events as they often have their own communication networks. Local newspapers and media are very good allies if involved from the planning stage. Norfolk's 'Treasure Island' initiative was sponsored by the local newspaper and there was the added advantage of extra publicity. The possibilities are endless. Co-operation may also be with large stores, local bookshops, theatres, cinemas, other council departments, centres for the disabled, and many others. A few years ago Sheffield Libraries held an under fives fortnight. The initiative came from libraries but a planning group was formed comprising representatives from a dozen local organisations including the PPA. It so happened that this year was the Silver Jubilee of the PPA so they were also interested in promoting services to under fives. Events, organised by all these organisations took place all over the city. Theatres and cinemas joined in. There were activities and events in parks, libraries, theatres, cinemas, stores, nursery schools. Stores put on relevant window displays and took the opportunity to promote their facilities e.g. changing rooms for young children. The local toy shop lent a display of cuddly toys to the Central Library and all the local bookshops contributed.

The advantages gained from all this were shared resources to provide an event that had maximum impact. The local paper and the free papers had an item in every day of the fortnight, and the local radio station did numerous features. An added advantage was the links that were formed and information and feedback which enabled the system to improve services.

National Children's Bookweek is an example of co-operation on a National basis. Headed by the what was **Children's Book Foundation**, the week is synchronised and run by many authorities in Britain. The theme is set centrally and publicity materials such as posters, balloons, giveaways (e.g. stickers, bookmarks etc.) are usually available for purchase from Book Trust.

This leads to discussion of awards, grants and sponsorship. As budgets shrink, libraries are increasingly appealing for sponsorship and applying for grants. It is noticeable that such awards are becoming more difficult to obtain as competition increases.

Often it is money that is sought. This may be to sponsor events, publicity or outreach to special needs groups. Appeals may be to commercial organisations such as Sainsbury's or Lloyd's bank either locally or through central offices or sought from charities such as the BBC.'s Children in Need appeal. Rotherham received money from this source for their Rocket Readers scheme, a scheme designed to promote reading to reluctant readers. Regional Arts Councils often have schemes to pay some costs towards using local authors. Others in the book world, book suppliers or publishers for example, may also provide funding for specific schemes. Franklin Watts sponsored a county-wide book festival in Oxfordshire a few years ago. Woodfield and Stanley sponsored an initiative in Cumbria to promote libraries to deaf children and also met the costs of the publication of a publicity leaflet for school governors on school library services, produced by the Yorkshire Children's group. (a co-operative group of children's librarians from several authorities).

A word of caution here. Sponsorship is more complicated than it may first appear. True sponsorship may form a legally binding contract, and from the sponsor's point of view will be part of a business strategy. Accepting money or other benefits will bring with it obligations and conditions which the sponsor will expect to be met. There are many pitfalls e.g. are the policies of the organisation in line with those of the authority? The logo of the sponsoring body will have to be displayed on any publicity produced for the sponsored events. Is this likely to cause conflict or other problems?

Money or direct payment may not be all that is availble. Publishers often wish to promote thier own authors. Sometimes this may be an author from abroad. Both Judy Blume and Paula Danziger from the States and Margaret Mahy from New Zealand have done British tours. Publishers will often advertise for venues in journals such as the Bookseller and libraries have the opportunity of hosting these. Most publishers have publicity departments whom librarians may contact to discuss author visits, hire costumes and obtain biographical and promotional material about authors and their books. Suppliers may also sponsor or at least provide contacts for such events although there is a growing tendency for suppliers to host their own author evening. However they may be able to lend support in other ways such as providing contacts, helping with printing, or giving the benefit of their marketing expertise.

Such sponsorship may be at a much more simple and local level. Local theatres and shops may be willing to dispense with or lend window displays, costumes, sets and props which may help decorate libraries for events or displays.

Working with others usually means that more spectacular and far-reaching events may be staged than by a librarian working alone. Valuable contacts are made and above all it is often more fun. A word of advice is to involve any outside agency as soon as possible in the planning cycle and preferably at the planning stage. This ensures that both sides have the opportunity to consider and discuss the ideas which will afford maximum benefit to all organisations involved.

Professionally, over the last ten years or so promotion of library services for all, not just children, has gained respectability. In the 1980's the Publicity and Public Relation's group of the Library Association came into being as did the LA/T. C. Farries Awards. These reward individual and programmes of events and there is also an award to an individual for his/her contribution to public relations. Despite this, there is still a great need for professionalism and for the promotion of children's services to be justified and defended as an "integral part of service delivery".

## References
1. Library Association: Children and Young People. Library Association Guidelines for Public Libraries. London: Library Association, 1991.
2. Ibid. p.29
3. Ibid. p.9
4. Ibid p.10
5. Margaret Marshall: An introduction to the world of children's books. Aldershot: Gower, 1982. pp. 155–156
6. Library Association (1991): op. Cit. p.30
7. Library Association (1991): op. Cit. p.30
8. Ivan King: Promote! The handbook of public library promotions. London: Library Association (PLG). 1989. p.3
9. Library Association (1991) op cit. p.31
10. Library Association (1991) op Cit. p.31
11. Jan Pienkowski: Dinner Time. London: Orchard, 1989.

# CHAPTER 2

## PR & PROMOTION OF SCHOOL LIBRARY RESOURCE CENTRES

**Gwil Huws**

### A: rationale

Although professional librarians are faced with the enormous task of convincing the public of the value of library and information services in general this is nothing compared with the far greater need to promote school libraries. For reasons we do not have time to explore here the development of school libraries in the United Kingdom during the twentieth century has generally been very limited. Even today there are many examples of secondary schools which have invested very few resources in the school library whilst most school libraries remain under-resourced and under-funded and many have to double up as a classroom or meeting room because of a school's accommodation problems. Furthermore only some 10% of secondary schools have a qualified librarian in charge of the school library resource centre. The remaining school libraries are normally staffed by unqualified library assistants and/or teacher-librarians who are expected to fit this duty into an already busy schedule.

In view of this background to school library development in the United Kingdom it might appear strange at first that Ann Irving, in her recent pamphlet on marketing information and library services, sees school libraries as being the most effective means of improving the image of librarians in general:

> '. . . we are seriously failing to market ourselves and our services to a wide range of people who exert influence on our national infrastructure, and thus the development and extension of our profession . . . I believe that changes in the way we interact with the educational process will have a long-term influence on how we are perceived by all of society. Society's images of what we do, who we are, and what knowledge and skills we possess, are formed from a variety of experiences, many of which are drawn from the influential childhood years.' (1)

However, the logic of her argument is based on the premise that 'most library and information professionals hold some responsibility for helping their customers to develop and use information skills' (2) a task which links librarians together. Irving claims that as this is already a highly developed activity in school libraries it would seem sensible to use it as a basis for projecting an improved image of librarians in the emerging information society.

Planning and conducting effective promotional activities and PR for any product organization is both expensive and time-consuming and as most schools in the United Kingdom have limited budgets. Headteachers and school governors are unlikely to fund activities simply to improve the image of the library profession. Justifiction for funding activities to promote the services and collections of the school library must, in the first instance, be based on a belief that these libraries have an intrinsic value which deserves to be promoted. However, before we can fully appreciate the value of school library resource centres it is necessary to understand the mission of schools in general and then consider the contribution that school libraries are making in order to ensure that their parent body achieves its stated mission. Official statements on the school curriculum during the 1980s suggested amongst other thngs that the purpose of learning in primary and secondary schools was to help pupils to develop enquiring minds, to learn how to use language effectively as well as to acquire the knowledge and skills needed to live in today's society. The following statement from *The curriculum* 5–16 summarizes the mission proposed for schools:

> 'A school's curriculum consists of all those activities designed or encouraged within its organisational framework to promote the intellectual, personal, social and physical development of its pupils.' (3)

It is worth comparing the statement above with the opening quotation of Chapter 1 to see that there is little to distinguish between the basic philosophies behind them.

The close link between school libraries and learning has received considerable attention in professional literature published during the past fifteen years. For example, the International Association of School Librarianship recently published a policy statement on the functions of school libraries which opens thus:

> 'The school library media center functions as a vital instrument in the educational process, not as a separate entity isolated from the total school learning program but totally involved in the teaching and learning process . . .' (4)

Similar references pointing to the key role of school libraries in the educational process can also be found in documents produced nearer home:

> '. . . the school library has an essential and central task in the school curriculum and that library skills are its foundation'. (5)

and

> 'A well-run library is central to the learning process . . .' (6)

The rationale behind this new perception of the function of school libraries can be traced to the rapid changes which have taken place in education in recent years. For example, in England and Wales we have seen the introduction of GCSE, TVEI and more recently the National Curriculum. As the Library's Association's

Guidelines show there has been a change in the perception of the learning process which involves children taking an active part in their own learning which in turn 'requires a shift of emphasis from the learning of facts to the development of skills and an understanding of the processes of learning' (7). As a result of this shift in emphasis, learning to learn and the handling of information have begun to be seen to be as much a part of the school curriculum as knowledge content.

In addition to providing and organizing relevant learning materials, the single most important contribution that school library resource centres and staff can make to the development of autonomous learners is through their contribution to information skills teaching. As suggested in the recently published LA guidelines:

> 'At the heart of any pupil-centred learning activity is a sequence of tasks requiring pupils to locate, select, interrogate, interpret and communicate knowledge and understanding.' (8)

This in turn 'brings library and information services into the centre of the delivery of the curriculum and into the centre of the learning process.' (9)

One of the main contributions of the staff of the school library resource centre towards supporting the learning process is to advocate an integrated information skills programme across the curriculum. Where such programmes exist, activities planned by the librarian and teachers cooperatively are one of the most effective ways of promotion with both teachers and students. Even in those schools where the integration of these skills has not yet been achieved, the provision of locational skills by the library staff still plays an important part in promoting the facilities and services available to students.

Unfortunately, most school library resource centres in the United Kingdom have some way to go yet before it can be said that they play a central role in the learning process, but there is a responsibility on school librarians to do their utmost to ensure that an awareness of the changing role of school libraries is communicated effectively both nationally and in individual schools. Librarians must not assume that there is general understanding of this enhanced role for school library resource centres, despite publications such as the 1984 LISC report and the 1992 LA guidelines. Also, empirical research which evaluates the contribution of school libraries to students' learning is short on the ground especially in the United Kingdom. A recent review of research on the relationship between academic achievement and school library provision in the United States shows that what little research exists in this area suggests that students' academic performance is improved in schools where a central library and a professional librarian are to be found. (10)

One of the conditions which are needed for a more positive image of school library resource centres is a clear statement of their purpose. Fortunately, this need has been addressed during the past few years both by the School Library Association and the Library Association.

The SLA for example produced the following list of functions:

1. Resource Provision
2. Promotion of books and reading

3. Information skills teaching
4. Guidance
5. Resource organisation
6. Information retrieval
7. Curriculum support and enrichment
8. Accommodation for learning (11)

A similar list of functions was produced by the Library Association in its recent guidelines:

1. To assist in providing a comprehensive source of learning materials in different formats for use by pupils individually and in small groups ... to satisfy curricular, cultural and supplementary requirements.
2. To organise all relevant learning and teaching materials within the school, providing a centralized information system concerning all the learning resources available in the school ...
3. To act as liaison with outside agencies and information services and encourage their use by pupils and staff.
4. To acquire and disseminate comprehensive information to all staff on materials to meet professional needs and, in cooperation with them, to be actively involved in curriculum development ...
5. To make its team available for teachers to consult on the selection and use of appropriate material to achieve their learning objectives.
6. To make opportunities for staff and pupils to learn how to use relevant materials, and provide training in the exploitation of the facilities of a school library resource centre.' (12)

Both sets of guidelines confirm the intrinsic value of school libraries in relation to the mission and goals of the schools which they aim to serve, thus justifying the need to conduct promotional activities which will enable all members of the school community to become aware of the 'products' and services which are offered by school library resource services.

Although there is much in common between the two sets of guidelines there is a more direct reference to the importance of promoting books and reading in the SLA's list. Emphasis on this function has been overshadowed in the literature on school library resource centres during the past few years by developments in information technology and information skills teaching. Fortunately, practising school librarians continue to perceive developing the reading habit as a major part of their role. Encouraging books and reading, whether for recreational or utilitarian purposes, remains an extremely vital element in the intellectual and emotional development of young people, and thus it is important that the school library resource centre continues to promote reading at every opportunity. In fact, a young person's success in reading has an immeasurable effect on the development of an individual's personality, information skills development and general intellectual capacity:

'Children who are successful (in learning to read) ... tend to develop feelings of autonomy, mastery of the school environment, positive attitudes towards learning, favorable attitudes towards school and realistic appraisals of their achievement. They also believe in their inner control over school success, that effort and their own ability will make the essential difference . . . These attitudes combine to produce a positive self image and continuing motivations'. (13)

Evidence exists which suggests that one of the most important conditions required for young children to master the skills of reading and for older children to develop a life-long reading habit is access to a wide range of reading material, either in the home and/or at school, particularly when linked to a conducive reading environment. This, for example, was one of the main findings of the Bradford Book Flood Experiment conducted in the late 1970s. Both of these conditions should be available to all pupils, regardless of age, ability or background, through their school library resource centre.

The librarian, therefore, has a responsibility to do everything possible to see that these conditions are available to all pupils. Having established the vital role of school libraries in the educational process and their contribution towards enriching young people's lives through their materials we need look no further for justifying any investment of time and money in their promotion.

## B: public relations and promotion strategies

In the second part of this chapter we shall identify the most important groups who should be targeted by PR campaigns and promotional activities.

It may first be worth noting the importance of the role and status of the school librarian to any promotion planning. Evidence exists which suggests that there is a close correlation between the perceived and the actual status of the school librarian and the role performed by the school library:

> In order to interact with teachers effectively and to participate in curriculum planning, whether as information skills consultant or, more usually, advising on the availability of resources, at least assistant-teacher status for the librarian was required. Many teachers and librarians felt that a higher standard than assistant-teacher would be more appropriate and that head of department more accurately reflected the responsibilities that were expected. (14)

This implies that establishing an appropriate role for the school librarian in the school's management structure could play a significant part in promoting the library services.

Whatever the status of the librarian any promotion and PR should be carefully planned and targeted.

> 'Effective public relations includes targeted communication strategies, sending the right message to the right audience.' (15)

If we accept the notion that promotion and public relations activities follow on, form and are secondary to the marketing plan and that 'Marketing is . . . basically involved with planning an approach to meet the needs of a potential customer and then bringing the customer and the product together in order to facilitate the exchange between them' (16) then it must follow that any promotion of the school library must be based on an understanding of the information needs and the interests of the community served as well as their attitude towards the library.

Planning for a public relations campaign should begin with a series of questions to establish what is the school community's perception of the role of the school library resource centre, whether they are satisfied with the services provided and what are their attitudes towards the library. Once the answers to these questions have been ascertained it is possible to formulate objectives for the PR and promotion activities which might well include:

a. to improve the community's awareness of the contribution of the school library resource centre in the learning process;
b. to improve the community's perception and confidence in the professional competencies of the school librarian;
c. to promote the advantages of using the materials and services provided by the library.

The next stage in the process would be to decide on the various strategies which could be effective. These might include activities such as library instruction, staff meetings, special events, exhibitions and publications.

In school libraries there are various groups of customers and potential customers— not only students, but also teachers, administrators and quite possibly parents and the wider community. But even within these groups there are different information needs and interests which must be catered for, e.g. students from different cultural/linguistic backgrounds, reluctant readers, students with learning problems. An effective marketing strategy for a school library resource centre, therefore, should begin by 'identifying a number of markets or a number of segments within the one market' (17), establishing their information needs and their attitudes towards school libraries and finally identifying the objectives of the promotional programme which should be targeted at them.

Before we consider what are the market segments to be targeted by school library resource centres we need to be aware of the importance of effective communication and interpersonal skills to PR and promotion. The importance of good communications to enhance the development of sound interpersonal relationships between librarians and their users, particularly teachers, has been emphasised by many authorities such as Kulieseid:

> 'Increased communication can contribute to the development of more cooperative relationships, whereas isolation and lack of shared information can lead to competition rather than collaboration.' (18)

Without good interpersonal skills all strategies to promote school library resource centres are likely to fall on deaf ears.

Let us now consider the most important market segments which school library resource centres should target, how this should be done and why.

**–Promoting the school library resource centre to teachers**
Attention has already been drawn to the fact that many teachers have little, if any, understanding of the functions which should be performed by school libraries or

that school librarians possess skills which could support teachers in their work. This low perception and lack of understanding of school librarians has to be removed before any progress in developing school library resource centres as learning laboratories can be achieved.

Strategies to raise teachers' awareness of which resources are available in the school library and how school librarians can support their work could include in-service training courses organised by the school librarian on themes such as information technology in libraries, information skills, trends in literature for young people, as well as regular reports on activities/services to staff meetings.

Other approaches which could be employed to promote the school library amongst teachers might be more informal and conducted with individual teachers. For example, the school librarian could initiate a dialogue with a teacher suggesting how the materials available through the school library resource centre could be exploited to achieve certain learning objectives in his/her subject field. This could be done either by circulating select lists of library materials to the teacher concerned or talking informally with individual teachers whose curricular responsibilities are known to the librarian.

Another approach might be to draw the attention of teachers to resources relevant to their teaching which could be purchased through the school library resource centre. This might involve circulating standard bibliographies, publishers' catalogues, review journals etc. to members of the teaching staff, obtaining preview copies or arranging visits to library suppliers or specialist bookshops. Although this is by no means an exhaustive list of methods it illustrates the importance of the librarian taking a proactive role to demonstrate to teachers the relevance of the library and its collection to their work.

However, the single most important strategy for promoting the school library resource centre amongst teachers is through good interpersonal skills. As we have seen, one of the most difficult obstacles facing school librarians is the low perception of them held by many teachers. Overcoming this difficulty should never be underestimated, but it is absolutely essential that this is accomplished before embarking on any promotional activities targeted at teachers. This means not only that school librarians require good communication skills, but that they should also strive to be highly visible members of the school community in locations other than the library itself. Many practising school librarians have emphasised the importance of being fully accepted into the wider school community e.g.:

'The status of the librarian will be enhanced if he or she is seen to play an active role in the life of the school. Informal relationships are also developed and strengthened.

(Qualified librarian)

It is important to play a full part in the life of the school: be a governor, run a marathon, act daft in the school pantomime ...

(Nottinghamshire qualified librarian)' (19)

Being visible in informal settings, such as the school staffroom, can also be vital for breaking down barriers between the librarian and some teachers but only if the librarian is a good listener and is willing to be patient to await suitable opportunities to canvass the library's services and resources!

### –Promoting the school library resource centre to students

Whether the school library is merely a storehouse or has evolved into a centre fully integrated into the school curriculum, there is a responsibility on the school librarian to promote the library's collections, facilities and services to the pupils. If the collection is relevant to their curricular and leisure pursuits it is vitally important that they exploit them fully. Experience has shown that providing such materials and services is no guarantee that they will be used.

One of the most difficult tasks facing many school librarians is how to break down the many barriers which might stand in the way of the pupil. These barriers may include lack of awareness of the resources offered by the library, its location, its layout, too formal an atmosphere, unfamiliarity with library procedures, unhelpful, confusing retrieval system, unsuitable or unattractive materials, reluctant readers etc. Whatever the obstacles it is the librarian's responsibility to identify them and to try to remove them. Strategies available for this might include formal orientation sessions on the library layout and procedures, informal reading and viewing guidance for individual students in relation to their curriculum and recreational needs and a range of activities such as storytelling sessions, book weeks etc.

Equally important for promoting the library with this group of users and potential users are features such as an atmosphere which is conducive to both learning and recreational activities.

Other conditions which would project a favourable image of the school library resource centre include central location, generous opening hours, relevant and balanced collection of materials, quality information service and friendly and approachable staff. Above all the school library resource centre should communicate constantly to students that one of its chief aims is to be responsive to their needs and interests.

Clearly, students will develop a more positive attitude towards the library resource centre if it is perceived by them not only as a vital resource for school and personal needs but also as an area for relaxation and fun. This is why many school libraries organize clubs, quizzes and competitions, etc.

### –Promoting the school library resource centre to the headmaster

' . . . when programs compete for scarce resources in the school, only those which can demonstrate direct impact on student learning are safe from the budget axe. Those which are regarded as supports will not survive in lean times.' (20)

We have already drawn attention to the fact .at many school libraries are under-resourced. Without the full support of Headteachers, it is very difficult to see any significant improvement to their funding in the foreseeable future despite the fact that the learning objectives of the National Curriculum are unlikely to be achieved without better resourced school libraries. The task facing the librarian in schools where the support of the Headteacher of the library service is less than

100% is to convince him/her that it is a vital resource within the school and that support for the library will help the school to deliver a quality education for its pupils. However, because of competing demands for a share of the school budget, school librarians will need to establish a careful strategy to promote the image of the school library with the Headteacher through good PR activities.

The following checklist of communication strategies provides a useful guide to school librarians who may be unsure how best to approach their Headteacher:

'* Always highlight positive achievements . . .
* Do not presume that the principal knows the latest developments. Provide him/her with professional readings.
* Regularly schedule time to discuss current issues.
* Collaborate to draft policies, set priorities, and monitor progress towards goals.
* Encourage the principal to observe library resource centre activities.
* Submit brief reports noting in particular outstanding examples of cooperative planning and teaching.
* Advocate ways in which library resource centre services can meet the needs of the school's curriculum.
* Contribute to professional development activities.
* Where appropriate invite the principal to accompany you to inservice activities and professional meetings.' (21)

**–Promoting the school library resource centre to parents and the wider community**
'Beyond the benefits to the library program, public relations activities fulfil our obligation to keep parents and other taxpayers informed. They have a right to know what impact the library has on children's education . . .' (22)

Recent developments to increase the influence of parents and other members of the local community in the management of schools has increased the need for them to be informed of the role of the school library centre. By publicising the activities of the library through parnet newsletters, local newspapers and radio stations the library can project a positive image of its contribution to the school and to learning. Not only can this bring in much-needed additional funding through activities such as those organised by the Parent/Teacher Association and donations of cash or materials from individuals and local businesses, but it could also influence School Governing Bodies to see that the library gets adequate funding.

The main thrust of this chapter has been to provide the rationale for promoting school library resource centre services and collections as well as attempting to establish who should be the target of these campaigns and why. In conclusion it might be useful to present a set of guidelines freely adapted from those proposed by M. K. Laughlin suggesting strategies which could be employed when planning a PR campaign:

1. Public relations efforts must be preceded by a sound programme of school library resource centre services. Unless the librarian is convinced that he/she is providing a worthwhile product, it is very difficult to arrange activities and to produce publicity to persuade others of its merits.

2. In addition to being convinced of the value of the service provided through the SLRC, the school librarian must be able to articulate its goals and objectives as well as the potential for improved services.
3. Effective public relations demands careful planning.
4. Public relations must be a continuous process. Library staff should take every opportunity to make users feel welcome when they enter the SLRC, and always to be seeking ways to publicise the library and its services, particularly to non-users.
5. The promotion campaign should be planned to include activities/publicity targeted at the different market segments as it is almost impossible to reach all customers through the same activities/publicity.
6. When planning the public relations/promotional programme it is vitally important to consult the school's diary. This allows for cooperative activities with teachers and also avoids arranging events/publicity which will fall on deaf ears because it clashes with other significant events in the calendar.
7. School librarians should take advantage of all opportunities to co-operate with public libraries to promote the library and literature for young people.
8. It is possible to promote the school library resource centre on a daily basis by showing a willingness to satisfy the information needs of all its users. (23)

**References**
1. A. Irving: Marketing the Information profession to the information society. London: Library Association, 1990. (Viewpoints in LIS; 7) p.ix.
2. Ibid p.16.
3. Department of Education and Science: The curriculum from 5–16. London: DES, 1985.
4. School libraries in Canada, Winter 1989, 28–9.
5. LISC: School libraries: the foundations of the curriculum. London: HMSO, 1984.
6. School Library Association: Steps in the right direction. SLA, 1989.
7. Library Association: Learning resources in schools. Library Association Guidelines for School Libraries. London: LA, 1991, p.10.
8. Ibid p.10.
9. Ibid p.14.
10. P. H. Perritt & K. M. Heim: Enriching the standard curriculum IN B. Woolls. The research of school library media centers. Papers of the Treasure Mountain Research Restreat, Perk city, Utah, October 17–18, 1989. Castle Rock (Colorado): Hi Willow Research and Publishing, 1990, pp.70–71.
11. School Library Association (1989), op. cit., p?
12. Library Association (1992) op. cit., pp.14–15.
13. M. C. Robeck & P. R. Wallace: The psychology of reading: an interdisciplinary approach. 2nd. ed. Hillsdale (New Jersey): Lawrence Erlbaum, 1990, p.37.
14. P. Valentine & B. Nelson: Sneaky teaching: the role of the school-teachers' and school librarians' perceptions. London: British Library Research and Development Department, 1988. (library and Information research reports; 63) p.16.
15. J. Henri: The school curriculum: a collaborative approach to learning. Wagga Wagga (new South Wales): Centre for Library Studies, Riverina Murray Institute of Higher Education, 1988, p.63.

16. J. Henri: The school library program: a marketing approach. International Library Movement. 7 (1), 1985, p.35.
17. Ibid., p.39.
18. E. R. Kulleseid: Beyond survival to power for school library media professionals. Hamden (Conn.): Library Professional Publications, 1985, p.136.
19. P. Valentine & B. Nelson: Sneaky teaching (1988), op. cit., pp.19–20.
20. E. R. Kulleseid (1985), op. cit., p.136.
21. J. Henri (1988), op. cit., p.33.
22. A. Gordon: School library management notebook. 2nd. ed. Worthington (Ohio): Linworth Publishing, n1991, p.31.
23. M. K. Laughlin & K. H. Latrobe: Public relations for school library media centers. Engelwood (Colorado): Libraries Unlimited, 1990, pp.2–3.

# PART II

# GOOD PRACTICE

# CHAPTER 3

## PROMOTING LITERATURE AND POETRY IN NOTTINGHAMSHIRE LIBRARIES

**Ann Fairbairn and Tricia Kings**

Nottinghamshire is fortunate in being able to develop new and practical ideas for promoting literature because of commitment to training at all levels. Regular courses enable ideas to be developed and shared amongst librarians and also with non-professional staff who work on a day-to-day basis with children. A recent example was a two day training course, financed by East Midlands Arts, at which the poet Ian MacMillan, storyteller Hugh Lupton and the Storybox Team from Bradford College demonstrated ideas and skills which librarians could use in promoting literature.

Another important element in developing expertise is the opportunity to watch skilled professionals at work with children, and the programme of library promotions over the years has included writers, poets, storytellers and drama experts, whose techniques have been absorbed by library staff participating in their sessions for children.

There is often a perception by children, teachers and parents that books and stories in themselves do not make for interesting activities, and it often seems that children are not attracted into the library by the offer of a 'storytime'. These are often seen as a 'boring', passive experience, much less attractive than craft sessions, for example. A mini-survey among primary school children showed that storytimes were the activity least likely to appeal to them and that they would rather come to the library to write stories than listen to them. There was an obvious need to find a way to make literature more participative. For many children, as for adults, reading and writing are interlinked, and creative writing is a way in to developing an appreciation of literature. Moreover children must be free to attach their own meanings to literature and contribute creatively to the way a story is interpreted and understood. This means that how children respond to a story should be more open-ended, allowing more creative freedom to the child, and the possibility of alternative interpretations in discussion.

Currently there are several methods in which literature is being promoted in the country.

The *Nottinghamshire Children's Book Award* is an annual promotion, in which librarians select shortlists of eight books published during the year to promoted to under 7s and to 8–11 year olds. Children across the country are encouraged to read the books and vote for the one they like best. The promotion is sponsored by Dillons the Bookstore who award the prizes at a ceremony to which some of the participating children and their parents are invited. The promotion is run mainly through schools and its aim is to get children to read and discuss the books in school and with their parents.

This year it is linked to a competition in which children either have to design a pet, or write a story, depending on their age.

*Poetry promotion* has developed in Nottinghamshire over a number of years but began with a county-wide 'Feel That Beat'. Before the promotion, library staff took part in a half-day course with local poets and teachers on how to run poetry workshops. As a result of the peotry sessions which staff ran during the week, a poetry promotion pack was developed. The ideas are all simple and effective and mean that poetry sessions can be run for visiting classes and may be introduced into holiday activities for children. Mansfield District ran a 'Poetic Licence' fortnight of adult and children's poetry activities, with visiting poets and workshops run by staff. There was also a Poetry Poster competition which attracted a lot of entries from both adults and children. This competition will continue into the summer for children throughout the county and be a focus for work with schools and for holiday activity sessions.

1992 was 'Year of Literature' for Nottinghamshire and an important theme was *storytelling*. Many staff have been influenced by visiting storytellers and by the rapport they developed with their audience. Storytelling skills are useful in holiday activities and on the holiday mobile where there are audiences of children of mixed ages and abilities. Storytelling rather than reading can be particularly effective in holding the children's attention and can introduce them to narratives which are more direct, less trivial, and have a more emotional content than many stories in picture books. While listening to a storyteller children are building up their own visual images and are left with an experience which is often more powerful than a story read from a book.

*Storytrails* are a way of making a book the focus of an activity, either with a class of children, or during holiday activities. Generally short books are used, either picture books or books about the length of one of the 'Jets' series. Longer novels can be used if entertaining extracts are read.

'Solomon's Secret' by Saviour Pirotta proved to be an interesting book to use for a storytrail, ideal for introducing stories and games from other countries. Children could look for different animal prints around the library and see which country they would lead to. Another book used is 'Something Old' by Ruth Craft which provides opportunities to discuss old artefacts, playground games and traditional stories, as well as dinosaur activities. Storytrails can use a 'story within a story' technique, involve drama, art and creative writing, practise information skills, and use games as a way of breaking up, building on and inviting a creative response to a story Ideally storytrails enable the children to become involved in and relive a story relying as much on their own imagination as on the skills of the animateur.

Opportunities to spend a lot of time promoting one book are not often forthcoming

Teachers have limited time for class visits, and holiday activities are usually run as single sessions and can be unpredictable in terms of the interest of children attending.

One longer novel which was promoted, 'The Afterdark Princess' by Annie Dalton provided the opportunity for children to make their own 'Observer's Book of Monsters' and to draw maps of their own imaginary kingdom.

Sometimes parts of stories can be adapted to 'Choose Your Own Adventure' format, with a large map for children to look at, from which they can choose from several possible ways in which the story might develop. Or the map can be a framework for other stories and games located at different points of the map. This technique has been used successfully with 'The Enchanted Palace' by A. Bhatty-charia, where the map game introduces a choice of adventures for the prince before he comes to the enchanted palace.

'The Jolly Christmas Postman' by Allan & Janet Ahlberg also adapts well to this formula: the postman has to navigate himself successfully round a land of fairy tale and nursery rhyme to deliver a letter to Father Christmas, with children recalling the rhymes and stories featured on the map.

As expertise is developed in different ways of promoting literature, staff are finding that the emphasis on the traditional 'Story & Craft' session is lessening. With less staff time available for preparation, and less money for materials, more use is made of packs of books and ideas used successfully by other staff. Pooling expertise becomes more and more necessary as budgets become tighter but the change has not led to less exciting activities. In fact staff are becoming more confident in their ability to create interest among children, with developed skills, fewer materials, and a time-saving approach to preparation. The most important element however is the emphasis on children themselves and the creative energy which they can bring to these literature-based activities, making them ultimately more valuable and satisfying for everyone concerned.

**Involving children in the experience of literature**
These are a few suggestions of ways in which activities can help children to involve themselves in a story.

**Awakening curiosity**
To start with, how can you get a child to approach the story with interest and curiosity? One way is to use the unexpected—to show them an object central to the story, or a picture, or play a piece of music. Then try to get them to guess how it might fit into a story. Another way is to read the beginning, or an exciting paragraph, or a description of a character, and ask the group how they think the story might develop.

## Using the visual imagination

I find that I prefer not to show the children pictures from a story, or the cover of the book, but rather encourage them to use their own imagination to picture the story as it is happening. Storytelling rather than reading stories helps to encourage this also.

One way of encouraging the child to response artistically to the story is to introduce an activity in which they have to draw a character, or something happening in the story, and compare the way each child has a different image, each one equally valid. For instance, in reading 'Fatbag' by Jeremy Strong, I make sure that the children don't see the cover, and after the first chapter get them to draw what they think Fatbag looks like, using the clues from the story.

For older children, drawing a map of where the story is taking place, and where each event happened, perhaps adding events and locations from their own imagination, is an interesting way of comparing the different ways people see things.

## Appreciating the language

Writing activities with the children can be a way of focusing attention on the language of the story. Poetry activities can be carried out with a large group, or with smaller groups. Children can pick out words or phrases and rearrange them into poems. One interesting exercise is to get the children to pick out 6 words from a passage from the story, then add six words of their own, and rearrange them until it sounds interesting. Books with original use of language, such as those by Margaret Mahy and Joan Aitken, or Pat O'Shea lend themselves particularly to this exercise.

Poems can also be turned into songs, by setting them to a well-known tune.

## Identification with characters

Discussion can be used to get children thinking about the characters, whether they would have behaved the same in their situation, predicting what they might do next, imagining what they might be feeling. Make sure that you ask open questions, rather than just asking for a yes/no answer. Respond positively to all contributions, so that everyone feels happy about joining in the discussion.

Children could work in small groups to discuss how a character might behave in a certain situation, solve a particular problem, or express feelings about their situation.

Drama is another way of getting children to identify with characters, dramatising part of the story, retelling the story with children miming the characters, or using masks or puppets.

## Plot—participation, prediction and evaluation

Discussion again is a useful tool in getting children to think about what has happened and what might happen. Games are also interesting to use, partly to get children moving as a rest from listening, partly as a way of getting them to think about the plot and feel part of it. One particular game that I use is to draw a map of part of the story, with a small adventure at each location. Children can then decide which way the hero/heroine should go through the map, and vary the story according to their choices. This is a visual kind of "Choose your own adventure", and you can arrange it so that the end of the game fits into the next part of the story.

You can also get children to play or make a board game based on a story. Many party games can be adapted to fit into the context of your literature session. Children could mime a character for others to guess. You could play twenty questions based on objects from the stories. With younger children you can wrap up objects from the stories and get them to try and guess what they are from the shapes.

Younger children can participate in telling the stories if they have some kind of repetitive refrain. This makes them feel part of the story. Older children can be encouraged to make up their own stories based on the plot of a story they have heard. Or they could retell the story taking a different point of view.

**Retaining a memory of the story**
Many of the activities mentioned above can be used as follow-up activities allowing children to respond actively to a story: writing poetry, writing their own versions, getting children to retell the story, making board games, dramatizing the story, retelling it with face painting, masks, or shadow puppets, getting them to make individual pictures or group friezes, making their own books, making pop-up pictures or "Jolly Postman" style books with words, pictures, and things hidden inside envelopes. The writing, games and pictures can be kept in the library, to be used for display, played with, or made into books which can be borrowed by other children. In this way the children are contributing not only to the story but to the library.

In order to appreciate literature and understand what it can contribute to their lives, I feel that children need to see themselves as writers, or involved in some way in the creative process. Children are often not articulate enough to be able to respond to a good piece of fiction by just talking about it, or writing a review. But they can use what skills they have to make a creative response, through poetry, imaginative writing, art, music or drama. This helps them to evaluate what the story means to them, and incorporate the experience of literature into their lives.

**A few examples**
**Designing a storytime for younger children**
Using a "Storybag" or "Storybox" you can weave several stories, poems and games together, allowing the children to participate in the session. Make a list of stories poems and games which you know. For each one, find an object that relates to it. Put them all in a bag or box. Choose children from the audience to pick out an object which will introduce the next activity.

Games that you can use are singing/action games such as "There was a princess long ago", or "The farmer's in his den". Games to get children listening are "Rubbish"—retell a familiar story such as Three Pigs but introduce deliberate mistakes. Get the children to shout "Rubbish" each time they spot a mistake. This is a good game for breaking the ice, or wearing out their voices. In "Silly statues" children have to walk round, and when you shout the name of a character or object, they have to freeze, miming whatever you shout.

Traditional playground and street games are also good ways of getting children moving and participating. The new "Can I play" books by Jill Paton Walsh are useful in this respect, but you can use "Children's games in street and playground" by the Opies as well.

Another sessions could be designed using the "Magic 3" theme—telling folktales in which 3 objects appear, such as "Teeny Tiny and the witch woman". As a follow-up, there is a bag with three unrelated objects inside. After a discussion about the objects, the children have to make up their own story linking the three objects, and using the pattern of one of the stories they have heard. This could be done in small groups, or as a large group activity.

## Storytrails: promoting one story or book to a class of children
Storytrails use the structure of a story as the framework for a literature session, making children feel part of the story by incorporating discussion, drama, writing, and other stories into the framework.

## The enchanted forest, by A. Bhatticharia

| Elements of the story | Activity |
| --- | --- |
| Description of Indian palace | Look at pictures of Indian palaces, and consider the architectural style and decoration. |
| Prince sets out on journey | Print a passport for the prince, using designs from Indian art, and making up suitable wording. |
| Prince's journey | Use a map game to allow children to choose where the prince should go, and discuss what might happen. |
| The prince sees the princess | Children can work in groups to make up love poems. |
| The prince breaks the spell | Children discuss in groups how the prince can achieve the task. |
| The wedding feast | Discussion of Asian weddings, food, customs, clothes, music, dance. Tell another story from India. |
| Look at the book: | Discussion of how different languages can be written in different ways. Children learn to write words in different languages. |

## Ging gang goolie it's an alien by Bob Wilson
A holiday activity suitable for large numbers of children from 4 to 6.

As the children arrive, paint some of their faces quickly to look like aliens. Good face paint is available from Theatre Zoo, Covent Garden, and you can put it on very quickly. Send the aliens to hide around the library. Those who arrive late have to be the cubs/brownies. Explain to them that aliens have landed and some of them are in the library. Teach them a few words of alien language, and tell them to go and find the aliens, make friends with them, and bring them back to the story area.

Start the story, and when you get to the bit about packing a rucksack, produce a rucksack and look at all the objects inside it.

Later in the story you can see how many of the objects they remember.

When you reach the part of the story where the scouts are singing round the campfire, do some campfire songs and creepy stories.

Later in the story you can get children to make their own badges, using double-sided sellotape and scraps of card. Of if you have small numbers you can get them to undergo tests of some kind (forfeits?) and award badges.

If there is time at the end, they can draw their own alien.

### Using a longer novel: The Afterdark Princess by Annie Dalton
Start by reading the first section where the characters are introduced. Discuss with the children which of the characters they think are most interesting, or who they identify with. Read on until Alice the babysitter is transformed into a princess. Get the group to make an "Observer's Book of Monsters"—each child to describe his/her own monster.

Summarize the plot up to where Joe gets the map. Use a map of the adventures of the book you have prepared beforehand. Play the map game, getting the children to decide which way Joe should go, and reading occasional extracts from the book.

Read the part where Joe meets the monster and the Emperor of Nightfall. Summarise the end of the adventure. Work on a poetry activity—either choose a passage from the book, and get the children to choose their favourite words to weave into their own poem, or take some of the images, such as "Sensible as brown bread and butter", "As boring as school rice pudding" and get them to make up their own images linking characters and food. Finish off by getting the children to draw their own maps, alone or in groups, of their own imaginary worlds.

# CHAPTER 4

## PROMOTING LIBRARIES AND LITERATURE THROUGH READING GAMES: RECENT INITIATIVES IN NORFOLK LIBRARY AND INFORMATION SERVICE

**Joan Emerson**

### A modest beginning

Norfolk came late to reading games. But from a modestly produced reading game featuring the Olympics as its theme in 1988, the summer reading game has evolved into an expected part of children's library events, eagerly awaited by many children, and much appreciated by many parents.

Our first reading game, the "Reading Marathon" in 1988, which cost the library service about £600, overtook all our expectations by being taken up by around 2500 children. It was an eye-opener to us in terms of the promotional possibilities that were attached to an event of this nature. If our very simply produced photocopied material could get such a reaction, with very little promotional activity, what couldn't be done with well produced, colour printed, much more attractive material and good publicity?

### Laying the groundwork

The following year it was decided to give a much higher profile to the reading game. The pattern that was set then, and found to work well, has been repeated in subsequent years. A working group of about six people, including some children's specialists, and librarians who work in libraries, chaired by the Senior Librarian, Young People's Services, did the planning, meeting only about three times before launching the event. It was always felt to be important to include librarians who, because of their service point experience, have a very good grasp of how workable, and practicable, any ideas would be to operate from the library counter.

This element, of making the reading game smooth and easy to operate in busy libraries, has meant that Norfolk's reading games have differed from those produced by some other library authorities, where talking in detail to the children about the books they've read, or expecting written reviews of the books is an important factor. That approach was felt to be too expensive in staff time, and impossible in an authority the size of Norfolk to operate evenly throughout the county. The line taken then and continued in subsequent years, was that we would run the reading game in all libraries in the county, including mobile libraries, and that we would make the game so easy to operate that staff would be happy to carry it out, with the result we hoped, that large numbers of children would take part.

## The planning process

From the second year on, the reading game has been a part of the annual co-ordinating programme of events for children in our libraries. The objectives for the annual programme have been:

To encourage library registration and use.
To instill a love of books and reading.
To educate in library and information skills.

In order to achieve the three objectives the programme has included different elements. The reading game itself plays a part in the first two objectives, with the booklist that always accompanies the reading game, and backed up by the purchase of multiple copies of the books being promoted. The booklist each year has followed the theme of the reading game.

Many of our libraries make a large promotional feature of the reading game posters and booklists, with the books on display, throughout the summer months. In most of the years we have produced a reading game, we have also run a competition alongside it. The competition has never formed an integral part of the game itself, but has always been an added extra for those who wish to take part. Every child who takes part in the game receives a copy of the game, and on completion receives a badge. It is not the case that only a few lucky prizewinners receive something free.

As a library authority Norfolk has no objections to a competitive element, though we are careful to ensure that all children get something from the game itself. Rather, we have used competitions as a device for attracting sponsors. It has been our experience that most sponsors tend to be more interested in the competition associated with the game, because of the publicity it engenders, than in the fact that we are attempting to promote books, a love of reading, and use of libraries.

Having a competition with the reading game provides the opportunity to hold a public event at the close of the reading game, to draw the promotion to a satisfying conclusion, get some press coverage, thank staff who have worked hard to make the promotion a success, and present prizes to competition winners. It also provides a public forum in which to thank sponsors for their support.

Other elements of the annual programme of events have included, for example, the production of a special booklist for teenagers, and, to work towards achieving the third of the objectives, quiz sheets and games for use in class visits to libraries.

The planning and organisation for the annual programme of children's events, including the reading game follows this pattern:

The Young People's Services Working Group decides to ask about four or five staff, in addition to the Senior Librarian, and Assistant Librarian, Young People's Services, to form the Activities sub-group to put the programme together.

48

The group first meets in November, and agrees objectives. Group members then brainstorm ideas for a theme around which the programme will be planned. A theme is agreed on, with a title for the annual programme. They then plan a programme which will achieve their objectives. And for several years, a reading game has been part of the programme. The reading game follows the theme of the programme, and after planning the content of the game, its title is agreed upon. Other aspects of the total programme are also planned, and members take away from the meeting work they will each do towards putting the plans into practice.

**The planning timetable**

November of previous year: initial planning meeting, with work assigned to members of the group, and other staff as appropriate.

December: second planning meeting. All assigned work is put together, and details of the programme decided. At this meeting the reading game is discussed and the following decisions are made:

Who we will apply to for sponsorship.

What we want the format of the reading game to be, what shape, what size, what kind of paper, what (and how many) colours will be used.

What the layout, or basic design for the reading game will be.

What the text on the reading game will be.

What design will appear on the stickers, if using stickers.

What design, wording and colours will be used on the badges. What shape, size, kind of paper, colours, and wording are required for the poster.

What books we will promote in the booklist, and what the booklist will look like.

What quantities of reading games, stickers, badges and booklists are required. This decision is based on the figures for previous years, with an expectation that this year's figure will be slightly higher. It's less expensive per reading game to get all the printing done in one print run, but if that amount proves not to be used, it will have been more expensive than getting less printed originally. In practice, what has happened for the last few years is that the increase in the number of children taking part has exceeded the estimated increase, and a second printing has been done a few weeks into the game. We have always had more than enough badges made at the start of the game as they take about six weeks to manufacture, and to run out during the game would be a big problem.

We draw up a timetable for ensuring all components of the game are ready in time, while keeping sponsorship options open for as long as possible. We make sure that we know how long the printers require, and how much time we need to allow for the manufacture and delivery of badges, and stickers.

January of year of promotion:

We supply the graphic artists with our artwork and layout requirements for the reading game, posters, stickers, and badges. We instruct them that in their design they must leave space for any logos we might need to show, including our own, and we give the graphic artists a timetable for preparation of artwork, based on the timetable prepared for our own use.

February and March:

We have frequent consultations with the graphic artists, and make any changes we feel necessary.

We continue discussions with potential sponsors, and keep trying to get more sponsors.

We hold the third meeting of the planning group, to ensure that all is progressing satisfactorily.

April:

We order multiple copies of the books to be promoted.

May and June:

We complete all sponsorship negotiations, and having done so, supply the graphic artists with any sponsors' logos to be included in the artwork.

We ensure that all the artwork is ready for printing by the cut-off date, and that the manufacturers of the stickers and badges receive their artwork with enough time allowed for production and delivery.

We ensure, through various means, including team briefing, memoranda, and visits of Young People's Services librarians to staff meetings held for groups of libraries, that staff in libraries all over the county know what the reading game is about, and how it will work.

We take delivery of all components of the game, and distribute them to libraries, in priority order, ie posters, at least a month before the start of the game, and games, stickers and badges at least a week before the start.

We send out press releases about a week before the game starts. We make the books being promoted available to libraries. Librarians promote the reading game in schools.

July:

Start of the reading game.

Monitoring starts in libraries, with records kept of children taking part, their ages, and whether boy or girl.

Librarians continue doing promotional work in schools until the end of term.

August and September:

The game continues, and supporting events take place in libraries (story sessions, often with crafts, on the theme of the annual programme).

September:

The reading game ends, about a week into the beginning of term.

It will be seen from this timetable that a great deal of commitment to spending money on artwork is made, most likely before we know that any sponsorship will be forthcoming. We have found that as reading games get bigger, the planning has to be started earlier, and that for good quality artwork to be produced, the artwork cannot be rushed into a few weeks. We get an agreement that the library and information service will underwrite the cost of the reading game to an agreed amount, but that the use we make of this amount will be as little as possible, by obtaining what sponsorship we can, and in being careful how money is spent. This enables us to get ahead in the production of the game before sponsorship deals are made. The gamble we take is that the sponsor(s) will not want the artwork already produced to be drastically changed. Fortunately this has not yet proved to be a problem; to be able to show a potential sponsor good quality, imaginatively conceived and coloured artwork visuals can help in the negotiations for sponsorship.

## Using sponsorship

The second reading game, on the theme of conservation, and called "Worldwatch", was planned. We approached our local area office of the National Westminster Bank for sponsorship and had several meetings with the Public Relations staff about the project. From those meetings, we produced guidelines for discussions with later potential sponsors:

1. Always go to meetings with sponsors very well prepared. If it helps, practise what you will say before the meeting, and have facts and figures at your fingertips, including your costings for the game.
2. Be very clear to the potential sponsors about what you are offering them. Sponsorship is a two-way process; your sponsor will most likely want something in return for the sponsorship.
3. Listen to what the potential sponsor is saying to you: if you can see that a different approach might get you what you want, then adapt. Listen for the clue that will tell you what the sponsor wants to hear, and if you hear it and can use it, then it can become the "peg" on which you can "hang" your arguments.
4. Have prepared some areas on which you could compromise, but be very clear in your own mind on the areas on which you are not prepared to compromise. Use the former to your advantage, but stick to the latter.
5. Be convincing, but don't try to "con" the sponsor. You're probably dealing with people who have much more experience in the market place than you do—they're not going to be taken in.
6. Never offer what you can't deliver.
7. Tell your potential sponsor about any good media contacts you have. If you know that your local radio service has shown interest in previous promotions, tell your sponsors this.
8. Be open and honest with the sponsor about what the library service wants from this event. If he/she can see your point of view, it might help with a compromise you're both happy with.

The National Westminster Bank sponsorship was for money to pay for the game, but the partnership worked so well that they also provided two main prizes for the competition we ran for children taking part in the game, of weekends at Center

Parcs for the prizewinners, a friend each and immediate family. They also provided meals vouchers for the families for their weekend stay. The sponsorship by Natwest provided other good opportunities for the library service: the Director of Arts and Libraries helped with the judging of the competition, and made useful contacts for other sponsorship plans he had in mind.

Natwest's interest in our reading game was not in having their name and logo splashed over our promotional material. They considered themselves a household name already. The "peg" that could be used was their interest in being seen as supporters of conservation. Natwest had recently announced their national sponsorship for the Worldwide Fund for Nature, and our local branch was keen to be seen to be supporting the conservation-awareness stance taken by their national organisation. Of course it was a stroke of luck that we had hit upon a theme that interested them, on the other hand, in the theme for our reading game we were reflecting the very strong tide of interest there was in the country at that time for conservation.

## "Worldwatch"

The "Worldwatch" reading game was a walk through a wood, following the track made by a badger, ending at the badger's sett. At each stage children had to read a book (of their own choice, but borrowed from the library), write down the title of the book, and on returning it to the library, and showing their game card, receive a sticker featuring a paw print. Children were given a badge on completing this, having read twelve books. They could go onto the second part of the game, which took them around the world, with a quiz on the identities of some endangered animals. The competition involved writing and drawing about their idea for helping conservation.

From that competition, and from others we have run associated with reading games, we have found that however simple and straightforward you make the competition, there are some people who will make it much more complicated than it really is (almost creating their own extra rules!), and people who assume there has to be a trick question. In "Worldwatch" identifying the animals was intended only as an interesting extra for the children to do, and was not part of the competition. Details of the competition were very clearly stated, but a few parents complained that the animals were not clear enough to identify, and so it wasn't a fair competition. Despite all our protestations that the quiz was not part of the competition, there remained some doubt so we issued all libraries with the answers to the quiz to give to anyone who queried!

## "Treasure Quest"

The third of our reading games was on the theme of mystery and adventure, and took the form of a treasure map. The game was a little more complicated than following the track of a badger through a wood. We included some puzzles along the treasure trail, which was in two parts. The first part took the child from the Book King's Palace to the treasure castle. This involved reading ten books, and on reaching the treasure, there was a badge. If the child wanted to continue with the game, they could return to the palace, by an underground route, and receive a different badge on completion. For sponsorship we approached a local newspaper and although the promotion proved successful in terms of the popularity of the game, it proved to be a difficult promotion to handle with the sponsors. We soon realised that we faced problems not previously encountered. We had a meeting with the assistant editor, and colleagues of the newspaper we approached, and they were very keen on what we were proposing, said they would like to sponsor it, and make a large feature of the game in the newspaper. We were told we would hear from them.

In fact that was the only meeting we had with them, but we heard from the marketing manager of the "umbrella" organisation, who we discovered, was the man who held the budget for what our contacts on the newspaper wanted to do. From his point of view, he wanted the promotion (which he liked) to feature also in another of his company's newspapers. We liked the idea as it meant, of course, more publicity for the game, but the interest from our original contacts began to wane, as it was no longer their exclusive feature, and from then the heart seemed to go out of the sponsorship. It became evident that although the two newspapers were part of the same organisation, there was rivalry between them, and that worked against us. The newspapers did what they promised, and produced a full page spread on the game, did all the printing for us, paid for all the paper used, and bought the badges. But their interest was shortlived, contact was difficult, and the sponsorship agreement could not be described as a partnership.

Another practical problem that arose was that because the two newspapers had areas of Norfolk they each saw as their province, we had to have printed two versions of the game, the posters and the badges, with the different logos of the two newspapers, to be used in the libraries in these areas. This made the practical problems of distribution more complicated than it might have been.

The experience taught us another lesson in dealing with potential sponsors: try to approach the organisation through the most effective channel. In this case we were following up a contact that had been made, but it proved not to be the best entry into the organisation. The sponsorship would have worked better and more smoothly, if we had contacted the marketing manager for the "umbrella" organisation in the first instance.

We found that this game, although very popular with adults, and liked by librarians in other authorities, did give children some problems. They seemed to find it a little too complicated to follow, maybe because there were two maps, or maybe because there were too many words on the maps (for the puzzles). The number taking part in this reading game was slightly lower than in the previous year.

### "Exploring a River"

The following year the reading game was "Exploring a River". This was part of the annual programme entitled "Science World". We were very fortunate with finding sponsors for this. Norfolk County Council's Publicity and Public Relations Officer had contacts at the National Rivers Authority and Anglian Water. These organisations were approached directly through their Public Relations department managers, and a joint meeting arranged between them and us. This could only be arranged for 9.00am at the offices of Anglian Water, over 100 miles away. But if you're serious about getting sponsorship, you drive 100 miles for a meeting starting at 9.00am!

Again they liked what we were proposing, and now examples of well produced promotional material from previous years could be shown. This fact, with our proven success in a high number of the children taking part in our games, helped in the discussion; the sponsorship deal was agreed in a very short time, and all subsequent contact with the sponsors done by fax and phone.

Because the National Rivers Authority is the regulating body of water authorities such as Anglian Water, the two organisations did not want their logos to appear together, and so each sponsored different parts of the game. Anglian Water paid for the posters, and badges, with their logo, and the National Rivers Authority for the games with their logo.

The sponsorship deal proved to be quick to arrange, easy to manage, and was satisfying too, in its link with the theme of the game. It was good to get back to a sponsorship that was for cash. The sponsorship in kind done the previous year by the newspapers had been worth about the same to us in cash terms, but to be able to retain control over when printing is done, when badges are produced, and have the personal contact with the printers, and pick up a cheque when it's all done, is much less of a headache!

There were a few initial criticisms from staff that the game would be "too educational" to attract many children but this proved to be unfounded. In the event it greatly overtook "Treasure Quest", which was on a more "recreational" theme.

"Exploring a River" followed the stages of a river (a campsite at each), working back from the estuary to the glacier. For each book read a sticker was given, showing a tent. By now we had refined the reading game from experience learnt in previous years. We had reached the stage when we felt that the number of books to be read should be about ten. Some children will read more in the time, and can repeat the game if they want to, but for other children ten books to read in about twelve weeks is plenty, and seems to be about the right number not to be off-putting. The game now only had one part to it, and for the first time in our reading games we did not ask for any reviews at all. Reading games can work in different ways. One way is to run the game in a small number of libraries, and to target a limited number of children. This makes it possible for children's librarians to spend time with the participating children talking to them about the books and commenting on their reviews, and hopefully using the written reviews as a way of encouraging other children to try the books. Norfolk's reading games have not worked in that way. We wanted the promotions to be available to all our libraries, with staff in small part time rural libraries, and on mobile libraries, feeling as much a part of the promotion as staff in much larger libraries in urban centres. Inevitably with very large numbers of children taking part not all will complete the game, but we know from comments made by parents that many children take the game seriously and read all the books and really work for their badges.

## "The American Trailblazer"

The latest reading game Norfolk has produced was "The American Trailblazer", the programme theme being "America", because of the 500th anniversary of Columbus' discovery of America. This was a very attractively produced map of the United States, with ten places of interest featured.

Children were asked to read a book for each place, and on doing so, were given a sticker of a plane. On completion of the game they received a badge.

By now (1992), the recession was biting hard, and finding sponsors became more difficult. Companies with an American interest were approached, but with no results. Our only sponsor for the reading game itself was Askews Library Supply, who proved to be ideal to work with. They gave us a completely free hand in the production, design and organisation of the promotion, and imposed no conditions. It was greatly refreshing to have a sponsor who had complete confidence in us to produce a successful and professional promotion. After an initial letter of approach, all further discussion was done by phone. The reading game was very successful, with close to 14,000 children taking part.

Jarrolds, a Norwich based department store, was approached for prizes for one of the competitions ("Discover America" quiz) associated with the game. They provided specially produced tokens to be spent in their book department, and advertised the promotion in their store. Both they and Askews supported the prizegiving evening.

"Discover America" was a quiz for individuals or families, in which a set of questions was made available in our libraries each week through the six weeks of the summer holiday. We also provided a competition just for children taking part in the reading game. This was "A Postcard to the President".

The entry form was designed as a large postcard, to be completed with a message to the President of the United States, with a picture of Norfolk, England on the other side of the card. The fact that our prizegiving for this competition took place a few days before the presidential election in the States led to some press interest, with the focus on the advice the children were keen to give the next president. Prizes for this competition were books donated to us by publishers.

## Promoting the games

The reading games are planned to start in about early July. This is so that librarians are able to go into schools after the summer half term holiday to the end of term, to tell pupils about the reading game, encourage them to go along to their local library to take part, and to leave posters in the school. We have found our local schools to be supportive of our efforts, and keen to allow us to talk to children in their classes and in school assemblies.

About a week before the reading game starts we send out press releases to all local newspapers, radio and television services. Press coverage varies with each newspaper, some local newspapers showing great interest in what the library service does, while others show no interest at all. Where we have had great success with media coverage has been with Radio Norfolk, which in its programmes generally shows an interest in books, and lately particularly in the reading debate. In response to our press release we normally receive an invitation from Radio Norfolk to take part in a phone-in, to publicise our event, and answer listeners' questions about children and reading.

## Monitoring reading games
We compare issue figures for the three months in which the game runs, with those of the previous year, at each service point, and each year has shown, over the county as a whole, an increase on the previous year.

Children's issue figures in Norfolk have risen considerably over the last five years. There are probably several different factors contributing to this increase, in addition to reading games: an increase in the number of books children can borrow at a time, the opening of three new libraries, and of libraries in three village shops, and a general improvement in children's book stock around the county. It is, therefore, difficult to assess exactly what difference to issue figures the reading games alone have made. It seems that while the Reading Game is not the only factor in the rise of children's issue figures, it has had the effect of keeping up the rate of children's borrowing through the summer months, when it used to fall significantly, and when adult borrowing falls.

Our reading games are open for children aged 0–16 years with parents encouraged to let very young children take part, by having the books read to them.

We were interested in the ages of the children taking part. Over several years we have found that the pattern is like this:

Breakdown by age of child:

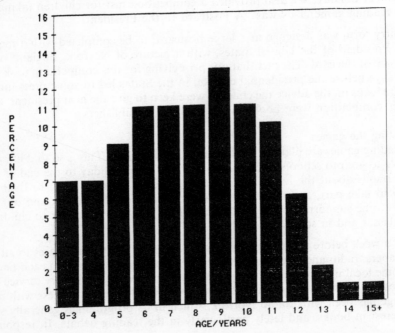

We were more interested in the widely publicised claim that girls read more than boys, so we monitored numbers of boys and girls taking part. Since doing so, we have consistency in our findings that percentages are: boys 45%, and girls 55%. Not quite the imbalance we might be led to expect!

By no means all children who start our reading games complete them. Some keen readers do the game several times, and others do not manage to read ten books.

The reading games have led to increases in library registration by children over the months of the game. In 1991 one of our larger libraries, which had over 100 children taking part, reported that over 100 children had joined the library in order to do the game.

### The cost of the reading game
Inevitably the cost of producing our reading games has risen with the large increases in the number of children taking part. With the sponsorship obtained each year the cost to the library and information service itself has decreased since the £600 paid out in the first year. The most cost-effective reading game was "Exploring a River". Including in the cost of the game all the artwork, paper, printing of games, stickers and booklists, and cost of the badges, the cost to the library service, after receipt of sponsorship cheques, was £39. (A unit price per child taking part of £0.36p).

In 1992 the cost of the entire reading game, with its posters, stickers, badges, booklists, posters for the competition, and competition entry forms was about £2800, for a promotion that reached 14,000 children, with sponsorship in cash and prizes covering a sizeable proportion of this.

The (uncalculated) cost to the library and information service has been in the time used mainly by the Senior Librarian, and Assistant Librarian, Young People's Services, though over the years, with the experience gained and lessons learnt used effectively the planning process and operation of the game has become fairly smooth.

### What next?
The danger will be that in subsequent years the same pattern might be used exclusively, and the whole exercise could become stale and lacking in new good ideas. The problem inherent in success is that more of the same is always expected. The need now is for a critical re-think. The probability is that we have reached a point where the number of children taking part is unlikely to be bettered. It's time to think about moving on to a different kind of promotion.

# CHAPTER 5

## LINKING SCHOOLS AND PUBLIC LIBRARIES—CLASS VISITS IN DERBYSHIRE: THE ALFRETON EXPERIENCE

### Ann Krawszik

Alfreton Library is a purpose built library opened in the mid 1970's. It has an open plan arrangement with approximately one third of its area housing the children's collection. The library has the advantage of a meeting room which is often used as a base for large classes visiting the library. There are two infant and two junior schools, one primary and one secondary school in Alfreton itself. In addition, there are several schools in villages surrounding the town. A good relationship has been established between schools and the library over the years. As a result of a wide variety of requests for general visits and for visits to achieve specific purposes, it was found necessary to structure class visits in a way that would enable teachers to appreciate the range of possibilities available. This approach also makes the most effective use of time spent in the library by groups of children.

### Why have class visits?

Class visits to the library are a valuable means of contact. They are an opportunity to meet groups of children and encourage them to use the library as individuals.

A partnership between the school and library produces reciprocal benefits.

Familiarity with the library helps

* to establish the library habit.
* to produce independent readers.
* to encourage enquiring minds and develop a life-long wish to read for pleasure.
* to give an understanding of the way in which a library is organised.
* to promote the library as a place of enjoyment.
* to de-institutionalise the image of the library in order to help children to approach staff and be confident in library surroundings.
* to support children's information needs in and out of school.
* to give children the opportunity to practise essential library skills. These skills are

59

locational, alphabetical, numerical and research skills. Reading, writing, listening and comprehension skills are also involved.
* to encourage teachers to use the School Library Service to support their work in schools.
* to encourage teachers to promote the public library to children in their care.

**What choice of class visit?**
Class visits can take several forms.

* One-off visits.
* Several visits for a set number of weeks with the aim of working with children on library skills etc.
* Regular time-tabled visits throughout the school year. Some or all of the activity options may be taken.
* Infant class visits are usually made up of basic information about library membership, story telling and browsing time.
* Secondary level visits are usually one-off or restricted to a limited number. The visits can be quite specific in their content. The library's role in the community, library organisation, sources of information are all subjects which often arise. Book talks to promote the teenage fiction collection are also an option.
* Junior visits to the library give a wide range of opportunities to promote the library and undertake library skills sessions. These sessions can be identified as

* an introduction to the library.
* information skills.
* information retrieval/reference skills.
* stories/reading for pleasure.
* fiction and information books together.
* book production.

**Preparation and Follow-up**
Establish through the teacher

* the age of the children.
* the numbers of children to visit.
* previous knowledge/previous library experience.
* the time allocated for the visit.
* what does the teacher want from the visit?

Discuss with the teacher the various options available and decide on a suitable programme. Also discuss the practical details of the visit, for example the times of arrival and departure, whether pens and paper are to be brought etc. After the visit(s) discuss with the teacher whether the session was worthwhile and appropriate to the children's needs. Respond to any comments arising and consider these for any future class visits.

**Class visits option 1: an introduction to the library**
This consists of three aspects: an introductory talk; a tour of the whole library; activities.

The introductory talk with the children is to establish what is already known about the library, to pass on information about how the library operates and to give basic information about membership and the services available. This time also gives the children an opportunity to get to know staff, ask questions and hopefully realize that libraries are relevant and have something to offer them. The danger is to give too much information at this early stage. The age, ability and existing knowledge of the children and the time available should be taken into account.

The tour of the library involves pointing out the main features and area of the library including both adult, junior and staff work areas. Appropriate items are demonstrated such as the photocopier, ticket laminator, computer issue and return desks. Large groups may have to be divided into smaller groups. It is useful to include the teacher in the tour. The time available and the interest of the children should be taken into account.

Activities include the use of a questionnaire called "What do you know about Alfreton Library?". This has simple questions based on the introductory talk and some questions requiring a search of the building: for example "how many clocks are there?", "which school has provided the art display near the picture-book collection?" etc. This allows familiarisation with the building and its layout. When there are large numbers of children involved it is advisable to start them off at different questions to avoid congestion in one part of the library.

A word-search puzzle has been devised which can be completed away from the library. There are questions about library membership and the library in general that have been discussed in the introductory talk. The answers are to be found in the word-search grid.

Another activity is to provide a basic plan of the library. Then the children are asked to mark where particular collections are on the plan. Alternatively, the plan can be labelled already with letters or numbers at appropriate places and the children asked to write down what is found at those points.

Alfreton has a collection of photographic slides showing different library buildings, services and activities. Selected slides can be shown in the meeting room.

An activity particularly suitable for a one-off visit aimed at promoting the services the library offers is a display presentation. This is when examples of items are provided and discussed and gradually assembled to form a display. Browsing time should be made available and some interactive equipment such as a fiche reader or date stamps should be included which the children can use.

Ask the children to walk around the library and make a note of what they can see people using in the library apart from books. Their observations can be discussed when they are back together as a group.

Especially on one-off visits, it is important to provide leaflets and basic information about the library for the teacher accompanying the class. Details of opening times and any other relevant promotional material are useful to have in school.

## Class visits option 2: information skills

Information skills sessions are usually offered to junior aged children of 7–11 years. The following ideas are possible activities which may be used in whole or in part or in any combination, depending on the outcome of discussions with the teacher. The activities are designed to be fun, build up confidence, familiarity and enthusiasm.

The aim is to develop children's abilities in using books, retrieving information and recording information with the aim of becoming independent researchers.

When explaining how information books are organised talk to the children and take them through the following:-

* What is an information book? Establish what constitutes an information book by giving examples and encouraging children to recognise the difference between factual, real things/people and imaginary events and stories.
* Identify the terms used- non-fiction, reference, facts, topic, project, subject etc.
* Compare the library to a supermarket ie similar products are placed together on the shelves. Explain how information books have a number on the spine. All books on the same subject have the same number on the spine and are, therefore, found in the same place on the shelves.
* Give examples. Show identical books and different books on the same subject all with the same class number. Explain that the name of the system is called the Dewey system. The story of Dewey is told in a light-hearted way in *Gawith, G. Library Alive!* A & C Black. 1987. 0713629002.
* Explain how the key to the information books' spine numbers is the Subject Index. Most of the subjects they may need will be found in there in alphabetical order.
* Practise finding words in the Subject Index. Include some subjects which are not in the index. Once it has been established that the word is not included, consider what other subject they might be found under. For example, making cakes (cookery), looking after kittens (cats) etc.
* Explain that the numbers which follow the subjects in the index are called "class numbers" and are important for finding books on the shelves. The numbers are in hundreds and the books on the shelves are in number order. Briefly explain the broad subject groupings:- 000- general/encyclopaedias/computers, 100-ghosts etc etc. Have examples of the range of subjects/class numbers available from 000 to 900.
* For older children explain the decimal point found in some class numbers ie this is because some subjects have different aspects and to make them easier to find each aspect has its own number. For example, European Countries 914, Great Britain 914.2, Germany 914.3, France 914.6 etc.
* Which is the odd one out? Read out a list of three or four subjects and ask the children to call out the odd one out. This exercise can also be transferred onto a worksheet where the subject which is the odd one out can be identified.

## Worksheet 1
If these books were on a shelf together, which one is out of place?

1. Trains, planes, ships, magic.
2. French, German, fishing, Spanish.

3. Dogs, light, sound, heat.
4. Butterflies, horse-riding, spiders, insects etc.

A worksheet on subject groups can also be used. This gives a list of subjects which are similar and the children are asked to name the main subject.

**Worksheet 2**

Christianity
Islam
Buddhism

Ships
Trains
Cars

Saxons
French Revolution
Elizabeth I

Worksheets can be used to give children practice using the subject index. Use subjects which are found in the index. For older children subjects can be identified which are not to be found in the index. They have to decide on an alternative line of enquiry and find a suitable class number.

**Worksheet 3**
Find the numbers in the index for books on these subjects.

Athletics    _____

Reptiles    _____

Chess    _____     etc.

**Worksheet 4**
Use the subject index to find the class numbers for the subjects in brackets eg: (dogs) 636.

1. The box took his (dogs) _____ for a walk.
2. The (castle) _____ is a ruin.
3. The (train) _____ leaves the station.
4. (Trees) _____ grow in the (rainforest) _____.     etc.

Use cards with different class numbers on and ask children either individually or in groups to rearrange them into the order they would be found on the shelves. Include whole class numbers with decimal points as appropriate to the age and abilities of the children. This activity can be transferred onto worksheets to give further practice in class number order.

**Worksheet 5**
Write true or false next to the following statements.

821 comes before 598 in Dewey order.
920 comes after 621 in Dewey order.

370 comes before 728 in Dewey order.
745 comes before 700 in Dewey order.

914.85 comes after 914.81 in Dewey order.
914.94 comes before 914.92 in Dewey order.
910.9 comes before 911 in Dewey order.
915.4 comes after 914.8 in Dewey order.

**Worksheet 6**
Look at the row of books below. One book is out of order; draw a ring around
it and indicate with an arrow where it should go.

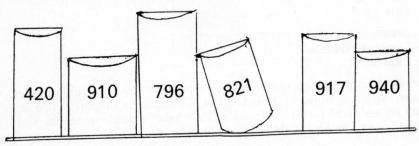

This can be made as simple or as difficult as appropriate. Other activities involve
practical work in the children's library. It is essential that the non-fiction collection
is in order before these exercises are undertaken. Write a subject on a card. Prepare
enough cards to keep a class busy and use subjects which are known to be
represented in the collection. The children can work individually or in pairs. They
are given a card with a subject on which they have to find in the subject index to
find the class number. Then they have to locate a book on that subject at that class
number in the library. Depending on the numbers of children participating the
searches can be checked by an adult or by having the children write down the
author, title and subject on paper. The latter slows the process down considerably
because after a few searches the speed of retrieval gets considerably quicker. With
a large class to-ing and fro-ing things can get rather hectic. Whatever method is
used, it should be stressed that each book should be returned to the place where
it was found. Some children like to count how many correct searches they make.
Scores can be compared at the end of the session. The benefit of this particular
practical exercise is that those children having difficulty with the procedures can
easily be detected and helped.

**Class visits option 2: information retrieval skills/reference skills**
This option aims to give practice in using encyclopaedias, other reference materials
and information books.

The research skills needed are retrieval, bibliographical, reading (including scanning
and reading in depth), notetaking and making sense of the answers.

Reference books can be one volume or multi-volumed works.

Small groups of children can be shown the different kinds of reference books available. For example, atlases, specialised multi-volumed encyclopaedias, the *Guiness Book of Records*, single volume reference books can be shown. Look at how each reference book is organised. Point out contents pages and indexes as appropriate.

Give each child a volume of an encyclopaedia and ask them to look through it quickly and find something that they did not know and which they would like to tell their friends. These facts can be written down and reported back to the class.

Sets of questions relating to specific encyclopaedias can be answered on worksheets. Questions can relate to one particular volume of an encyclopaedia or require several volumes to be consulted. Older children can be encouraged to find the answers to questions using the whole range of reference material. Quizzes of all kinds can be devised to make the process interesting.

Topic work initiated by the teacher can be undertaken using the books available in the library. This is most successful when the children have learnt how to find information and have practised retrieval skills.

Secondary level visits can involve more detailed looks at the various sources of information across the whole range ie books, newspapers, magazines, booklets, leaflets, organisations, TV and radio etc.

Study skills assignments can be used to get young people to look more closely at the library and be more aware of what is available and how the library is organised.

## Class visits option 3: stories/reading for pleasure

If the teacher would like the class to understand how stories are organised in a library, first establish what a storybook is. Give examples and encourage the children to name their favourite stories. Identify the terms used; for example, author, title, story, fiction, novel, surname, publisher, illustrator, illustrations, alphabetical order. Explain how books are placed on the shelves in bays and that storybooks are in author surname order. Explain and demonstrate how to follow the alphabetical order sequence around the shelves.

Various exercises can be undertaken to practise using alphabetical order which vary in difficulty depending upon the age and ability of the children.

* Ask for a volunteer to say the alphabet slowly and clearly. Compare alphabetical order to class registers. Stand the children in alphabetical order.
* Use cards with single letters of the alphabet on. Give a card to each child and ask them to re-arrange themselves into alphabetical order. To make this more difficult cards with two letters can be included.
* A selection of books can be taken, the covers from discards and book jackets for example. These can be given to groups of children who then rearrange them into the order they would be found on the shelves.
* A variety of worksheets can be devised to give alphabetical order practice.

For example

## Worksheet 1
Write true or false next to the following statements.

a comes before n in the alphabet
h comes after j in the alphabet
z comes after w in the alphabet
m comes before k in the alphabet

## Worksheet 2
Look at the row of books below. One book is out of order; draw a ring around it and indicate with an arrow where it should go.

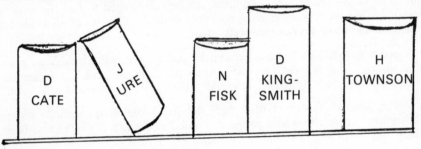

| D CATE | J URE | N FISK | D KING-SMITH | H TOWNSON |

## Worksheet 3
Look at the row of books below. Two books are out of order. Draw a ring around them and indicate with an arrow where they should go.

| B BYARS | A FINE | P CURTIS | G CROSS | R WESTALL |

## Worksheet 4

| A Davidson | R Dahl | A Davies | T Deary | A Digby | P Dickinson | E Dunlop | B Doherty |

## Worksheet 5
List the following books in the order they should appear on the shelves.

Dinner Ladies don't count by Bernard Ashly
Pongwiffy by Kaye Umansky
I am David by Anne Holm
Spirit River by Monica Hughes
How to stop a train with one finger by David H Wilson etc.

* Write some authors' surnames on large cards and then ask children to stand holding the cards in front of the class as if they were books on a shelf. The rest of the class are to check to see if they are in the right order.
* In the children's library use cards with authors' surnames on that are known to be represented in the collection. Each child gets a card and tries to find a book by the author and bring it back to be checked or writes down the title of one . of the books. The fiction sequence should be in strict author order before this activity. The children should understand why the books must be returned to the place where they were found. If the class has a large number of children divide them into groups so that some can be doing worksheets and others the practical exercise.

If the approach to fiction is to be reading stories for pleasure then the age and abilities and interests of the children should be taken into account.

* An activity which works well with infant classes is to use a story basket. This involves using a collection of toys and clothes which act as prompts for various stories. The items are then hidden from view and chosen by chance, or are on view for a child to select one. Then the story associated with the toy or piece of clothing can be read.
* Book talks involve talking to children about stories they have read and enjoyed and then reading from recommended books. Depending on the time available, short passages from books can be read or several whole books—usually picturebook format—can be read. Book talks can be random selections or centred around a particular theme, author or illustrator. Book talks work particularly well with secondary level visits. Books for teenagers can be promoted in this way. Bibliographical details of the books selected should always be made available.

Having someone else share the session and alternate in reading passages from five or six books, helps to give variety to the session.

Stories can be talked about in general terms in order to highlight the range of fiction available. Likes and dislikes can be discussed and themes apart from ghosts, animal stories and school stories can be brought to their attention. Have examples of each of these categories available. Ask the children to think of types of stories and then produce the example as they name them to make a display.

Include stories on sport, TV tie-ins, love stories, everyday life, history, myths and legends, ghosts, animals, classics, school, humour, short stories, science fiction and fantasy, adventure and mystery, magic, sad, cartoon format, choose your own adventure and picturebooks for older readers. Allow browsing time so that the children can discover more about the fiction collection.

* Children can get involved in reviewing. One author's work can be looked at. Provide a book display and a book list, giving bibliographical details. Read from the books and invite discussion.
* Look at one illustrator's work or compare several illustrators' work. Use appropriate illustrations by well known artists removed from discarded books or calendars etc. Back them onto card and present them in a neat and professional way.

67

The children can then try to find other examples of the illustrator's work in the picturebook collection.

* Formal review groups can be set up using books already in stock.
* Reviews for new books on approval can be arranged.
* Family reading groups are another way of encouraging wider reading and enjoyment of stories.
* Imaginative work can arise from stories. Read a story and ask how it could be ended in a different way or what could happen next. For example in Alistair's Elephant by Marilyn Sadler (Hamish Hamilton 1983 0241108098) what happens next after the giraffe follows Alistair home?
* Other activities based on stories can be stories on tape, stories on 16 mm film, making large floor books, writing stories for display in the library and various art/craft related activities.

**Class visits option 4: fiction and information books together**
Poetry is a useful link between the information and fiction collections. Poetry activities include reading poems, children reading poems, writing out poems and illustrating them for display in the library, acting out poems and information finding activities such a focus on facts session. This is a method of using fiction to initiate the use of non-fiction. Read a picturebook and then divide the class into groups to follow different aspects of the story. Each line of enquiry should be as diverse as possible so that the children are using different sections of the information library. The story should spark off lines of investigation which can be followed up in the non-fiction section.

**Class visits option 5: book production**
Sometimes children are interested in how a book is made. It is useful to reinforce the idea that each book they see has been created by a person and that it is not beyond their capabilities to do the same. If they can understand that books don't just appear out of nowhere, that they go through a particular process, then that may encourage budding writers.

Discarded books can be taken apart and examined. Different sized covers can be saved and compared. Publishers are often willing to provide material which they no longer need—such as proofs. It is interesting to ask the children when they write their own stories to make the story fit a particular format.

For example to make a story fit onto eight pages and have no more than x number of words etc. They then begin to appreciate the discipline of writing and can look out for common elements in the books they see. Linked to this activity is the possibility of inviting an author to talk to children about writing and books.

**Summary**
These approaches to class visits to Alfreton Library have been tried and tested over several years. They are continually revised and can be added to as new ideas present

themselves. There are many ways of introducing children and young people to a greater understanding of how libraries are organised and encouraging them to get the most from libraries. This framework of class visits options is just one way of bringing a structured approach to children's experiences of visiting a library as a class.

# CHAPTER 6

## WORKING WITH PUBLISHERS, BOOKSHOPS AND LIBRARY SUPPLIERS

**Linda Bennett**

Without a doubt, publishers are the big fish in the world of British books. Their "clout" is perhaps not quite as one-sided as it used to be—due to the fact that British bookselling became less fragmented during the 1980s after the rise of two major chains, Waterstone's and Dillon's, which are together responsible for approximately 25% of the retail book sales in Britain. Nevertheless, almost all of the big British publishers gain a significant amount of their turnover from overseas sales (and some of the biggest now have American owners). They are therefore cosmopolitan whales among booksellers who, if no longer parochial minnows, have still only achieved the status of brown trout—smallish, a trifle rarefied, and vulnerable to attack from rainbow trout—non-specialist retailing chains, book clubs, remainderers and others.

Library suppliers are biggish in bookselling terms, but they have less influence than the higher-profile retail chains. They are the eels buried in the mud beneath the political whirlpools. The reasons for this are twofold. Firstly, it is a question of choice—it is the raison d'etre of the library supplier to act as the neutral mediator between librarians and publishers. Playing politics is for him* a dangerous, potentially a lethal (*I use "he" as a generic term to represent persons of either sex!) game—if he were to venture into these choppier currents, he would not know from which direction the sharks might approach—they might even, ostensibly, be on his own side. Secondly, it is the result of his acceptance of the humble role in which he has traditionally been cast—he is a purveyor of books, a tradesman-figure. His opinions are not often solicited. (Significantly, only one library supplier has sufficient influence to persuade publishers to change book jackets because they probably won't appeal to librarians, though most could draw on their extensive experience and that of library customers to offer stirling (and free) "market research"—but that is another subject, and something of a hobby-horse, which I hope to deal with elsewhere.)

There is, however, an area in which library suppliers score highly, and in which they are perhaps regarded as more useful even than the highest-profile retail chains, because of their ready access to a wide range of informed and interested customers who will definitely show up on "the day"—that of author promotions. Library suppliers who want an author to help them to celebrate some landmark, such as the opening of a new showroom, or an anniversary in their history, or who simply want to co-operate with publishers in producing an "occasion", can usually be confident that they will be supplied with one of the current "big name" authors (a handful of whom exert even more power than the publishers!) if that is what they want—or perhaps with a group of "mid-list" authors who are experts on a particular theme or genre, if that is more appropriate.

Author events are fun, but they can also be a source of great anxiety. I will try to explain what they involve, and what, from my experience, the potential pitfalls are, in order to encourage more librarians to attempt them. The time, incidentally, is ripe for this—publishers are beginning to realise what useful and well-informed people librarians are. It is therefore not difficult for librarians to make arrangements for an author event with a publisher, particularly if they also liaise with a library supplier with a three-cornered event.

It might be helpful at this point to offer a brief history of the author events in which my company, the Woodfield & Stanley Group, has been involved. The Group consists of Woodfield & Stanley at Broad Lane, Huddersfield, the mainstream children's specialist suppliers, H. & A. John Booksellers at Normanton, adult and educational library suppliers with large paperback and hardback fiction stocks, and the Woodfield & Stanley subsidiary paperback showroom at Old Leeds Road, Huddersfield. Author events have been held on all these premises, as well as at the former paperback subsidiary in Scunthorpe. Joint events have also been held in libraries and other public places—but I will return to these later.

Our first foray into this type of promotion took place in 1977, and involved, not an author, but a 1200 year old book. The occasion was the reissue of the Book of Kells, in a sumptuous edition, by Thames & Hudson. The evening consisted of a presentation by editorial staff at Thames & Hudson on how the book was made, and the difficulties they had encountered in such matters as reproducing the original artist's colours faithfully. It was certainly the most erudite of all the evenings that we were to host, and remains among the most successful. This was followed in 1980 by a more "usual" type of event—the opening of the new hardback showroom at Normanton by Jack Higgins. Thereafter, H. & A. John's had an author event once a year. Guests of honour included Catherine Gaskin, Craig Thomas, Sue Townsend and Margaret Graham. The Scunthrope showrooms were opened by Helen Oxenbury. Other variations on the "straight" author evening included "An Evening of Romance" with Mills & Boon on Valentine's Day in 1985, and an evening designed to commemorate the quincentenary of the death of Richard III in 1983, for which I, in my then capacity of cataloguer, produced a catalogue of Richard III books in print, and at which the speakers were people eminent in the Richard III Society. Librarians particularly liked this evening, which was the only one that we have held that was not affiliated to particular publishing houses. (There are, however, sound practical reasons for always involving publishers, which will emerge.)

Woodfield & Stanley began to give author evenings relatively late, but have made up for it by averaging more than one per year. Increasingly, they have focused on presenting several authors, often from different publishing houses, on the same evening, and this has proved to be very effective, especially as children's librarians are usually well-versed in their subject, and gluttons for information! They have also hosted some very famous names. One of their most successful events was the opening of the Old Leeds Road showrooms by Allan Ahlberg, who turned out to be a star who held the other guests spellbound for the entire evening.

Now I come to the practicalities of indulging in activities of this kind.

First of all, it take a lot longer than you might expect. Publishers like to work well in advance, and they also have promotional budgets which tend to get used up towards the end of the financial year (though, confusingly, some of them work to calendar years for promotional purposes). It is therefore not too early to start "trawling" for an author six or eight months before you want the event to take place. You might have to approach several publishers before you find one who has an appropriate author with a book coming out close to the date that you have in mind. Authors will, of course, come to occasions when they haven't got a book coming out, but there are two snags involved here:

1. Publishers will usually only contribute financially to events which promote particular new books.
2. Authors are expected to expend themselves on promoting their new work free of charge. They may charge (and quite steeply) for appearing at events where this is not part of the "package".

Once you have agreed an author and a date with the publisher (and confirmed it in writing, so that awkward authors can't back out!), you need to make cost-sharing arrangements with the publisher. This is usually done through the publisher's representative, though he or she may bring someone involved in publicity from Head Office to see you as well. (The likelihood of this is in inverse ratio to the number of miles between you and London). Over the years, the arrangements that we have made with publishers have taken an almost standard form, viz:

1. Library supplier to provide the catering, the premises, and the guests.
2. Publisher to provide the author, and pay the author's expenses.
3. Publisher to pay for half of the catering and (usually) drinks costs (some publishers have preferred actually to give the wine, etc. themselves) upon production of receipts.
4. Library supplier to provide prominent displays of the author's books, with as much promotional material as the publisher can send. The library supplier usually pays for these books, but on a sale-or-return basis. The publisher frequently provides a fixed number of books (say, 20) to give to prominent guests who would like a signed copy, but don't necessarily wish to pay for it!
5. The publisher usually likes to receive a copy of the guest list in advance, and may add some names to it. The author is normally attended by four to six people from the publisher's head office, plus sales representatives etc.

One important note: not all publishers are good at paying their share promptly afterwards, and most will try to pay "in kind" (i.e., with books) instead. They will not insist on this if you refuse—it is up to you to decide which form of payment you find the most useful. (You may get more books for your money, so to speak.)

As soon as you have a definite date for the event, and well before you start sending out invitations, it is a good idea to start telling potential guests, so that they will keep the date free in their diaries. Almost all of our events have been held in the evenings, as our guests consist principally of librarians and teachers, who find it hard to get away during the day. It is also a good idea to make sure that the date doesn't coincide with some major local event. This has never happened to us, but I once went to a Hodder & Stoughton launch for Jeffrey Archer which coincided with some local elections, and was very poorly attended (an interesting irony!)

The actual invitations should be sent out about three weeks before the event is to take place. Much longer before that, and people tend to forget; much nearer, and you don't have time to chase up people who haven't replied. Always put an R.S.V.P. date on the invitation, and set it about a week before the evening. Make it clear whether or not spouses are invited.

This is where the fun and games start. I have never yet been involved in an author evening where I was not convinced the week before that the whole thing would be a failure, and that no-one was going to turn up. In fact, they have always been successful, and we have entertained anything from 100 to 200 guests. The trouble is, people are very bad at replying to invitations. So, one week before the big day, there is no other remedy than to prepare yourself for a mammoth session at the telephone with your guest list. It is, of course, important to have a reasonably accurate idea of how many people to expect for simple housekeeping reasons. Another problem that library suppliers encounter (which is perhaps not as significant for librarians) is that almost invariably we meet librarians afterwards who say that they would have been delighted to come if only they had known about it. Our difficulty is that in some authorities, there is a definite protocol involved in distributing invitations, which are supposed to be fielded by line managers, who then often forget to pass them on. There is in truth not much we can do about this.

At Woodfield's and John's, we have always relied on volunteers from the staff to do the catering. There are a number of reasons for this: they do it superbly well; they achieve a personal touch which outside caterers can't manage (for example, Jack Higgins waxed poetical about our "genuine" Yorkshire scones); and they make the money go further, which enables us to have more guests, and to give them a better time. The wine is usually bought on a sale-or-return basis from a local supplier.

If you are doing the catering yourselves, and you don't have prior experience of events of this kind, you are almost certain to over-cater the first time. All you can do then is to make sure that the more exotic delicacies you are offering are not tucked away at the back. Otherwise, you can only be philosophical, and trust to the good appetites of your staff the next day! (Though, to be more serious, anyone wanting advice would be welcome to contact Pauline Bond at H. & A. John's, who now has at least ten years experience of such occasions behind her.)

Items such as glass and china can be hired quite cheaply and without difficulty. The hiring arrangements should be made several weeks beforehand, but often the goods can't be collected until the same day, and have to be returned the day afterwards, so make sure that someone is lined up to do this. We have always asked a local florist to make displays for the showrooms, and put posies on the tables. If the guest of honour is a woman, we order a bouquet or a corsage for her. This date of about a week before is crucial for a number of other matters if you wish to get the most out of the evening. It is the time at which you should contact the local media (press, radio—television if you can, though we have never succeeded in pulling off this particular coup) and ask them to send someone to cover it.

Also at this time, if the publisher has not sent the publicity material (you can be fairly sure that he will have sent the books, but if he hasn't, bend his ear about that, too), now is the time to start making a fuss about it. By publicity material, incidentally, I mean posters, blown-up photographs of the author, giant books, extra jackets, etc. Occasionally, the publisher's publicity department has been known to send the publicity material with the staff accompanying the author. This is totally unsatisfactory, and should be discouraged because:

1. You are on tenterhooks beforehand wondering whether they will forget it.
2. You haven't seen it, and don't know whether it will be disappointingly meagre—but at this stage, you won't have time to pad it out with something you have devised.
3. In any case, you face the prospect of your staff scaling the walls and standing on bookcases to arrange the stuff after the arrival of your first guests. Unjustly, this makes you look inefficient—and is hardly conducive to producing the best artistic result.

You need to be in touch with the person who is looking after the author (usually described as a "publicity director"—they don't seem to have any ordinary staff in London publishing offices) and find out exactly what the author is prepared to do on the evening. Some authors are happy to give fully-fledged speeches, or even entertainments, like Allan Ahlberg; some prefer only to give a short address; and some (few) will not want to talk to the company en masse at all, but will be more comfortable walking round and addressing small groups of individuals. Any of these arrangements works, but you need to be prepared for what is going to happen in advance. You also need to know if the author wishes to leave at a particular time, so that you can make sure that he or she has met all the people you want them to meet during the time which you have. If you are meeting the author and the publisher's party from a train, make sure that you know the train times, that they have allowed enough time for any preparations they may need to make, and that you have taken enough vehicles to the station! (Sounds silly, but I once had someone travelling in my boot!)

On the actual day, you need to check and double check all your housekeeping arrangements. You need to make sure that all your staff are happy and confident about what they are doing. You need to make sure that your building is as clean and tidy as possible, that all the bookshelves look immaculate, and that you have some attractive and prominent displays of the author's books in place.

Our evenings have never followed a very formal set pattern, but you should have some idea of the order in which you expect events to take place. Usually we begin with a sherry reception, which starts about half an hour before we expect the author to arrive (say, 7.00p.m. for 7.30p.m.). After the author's arrival, someone from the company (the chairman, or one of the directors) makes a short speech, to which the author is invited to reply. (Authors who don't wish to speak just make a brief acknowledgement.) The author is then presented with some flowers and/or a small gift. By this time, most of the other guests will have had an opportunity to inspect the premises, so it is a good time to proceed to the buffet. We usually set tables for people to eat at, and after the author has eaten, take him or her to the tables and introduce the guests in small groups. Eventually, the guests will disperse around the building again, which gives the author the opportunity to look at the book displays, talk to the staff, etc. Most frequently, the author leaves before the other guests, and the departure is fairly unobtrusive. It can, however, be helpful to draw attention to it if it is getting very late, and there seems to be some danger of burning candles into the small hours!

On the actual day, it is quite frankly a matter of good organisation—which means paying attention to every detail. Since the publishers, the guests and, not least, the company's own staff are all devoted to the idea of making it a successful evening, you don't really have to worry that things won't "gel"—as long as you stick to the mundane practicalities of making sure, for example, that there was enough wine-glasses to go round. We have (touch wood) never had a failed evening, nor any major embarrassments.

Clearing up afterwards is, of course, an anti-climax, but as well as the obvious matters to attend to (returning the glass and china, distributing the leftovers, disposing of the debris) there are some important and less obvious things to do. I am sure that everyone's good manners would extend to thinking of writing to thank the author, but it is important also to correspond with the publishers, who may wish to receive the names and addresses of guests they met who were interesting or helpful. (And not to forget to charge them for their share of the entertaining!) Don't forget also to thank your staff, who are probably stumbling around glassy-eyed and wondering if it is worth feeling the way they do at the present moment.

What I have described above are the preparations and the course of events of an "ordinary" author evening. We have occasionally engaged in more unusual enterprises. One of the most successful of these was part of a sponsorship package. In common with most library suppliers, we like sponsorship to take the form of some definite activity, rather than the simple handing over of money. In 1988, as a result of a conversation at a weekend school at Otterburn on Sponsorship and the Arts, I discovered that Humberside Libraries were looking for sponsorship for a worthwhile project (yet to be decided) which would underline their involvement in promoting literature.

We arranged a meeting with their chief librarian (then Peter Ainscough) and their arts officer, and agreed in principle to do something together. By great good fortune, Paul Sayer, who happened to be a local author, won the Whitbread Award for his novel "Howling at the Moon", at this time. (Interestingly, it was the same year that "Satanic Verses" did not win the Whitbread, but by virtue of the publicity following its nomination, drew down the Ayatollah's wrath.) I went to see him, and asked him if he would be prepared to be involved in our project. He said that he would, and Humberside Libraries and H. & A. John's sponsored a lunchtime reading by him at Hull Film Theatre for members of the public, followed by an evening reception for librarians, which he also attended, in Scunthorpe Library. H. & A. John's provided the catering for this (with the staff, imported from Normanton, once again doing all the work). But the serious part of the sponsorship consisted in our paying Humberside Arts Studio (which was affiliated to the library) to design and produce a poster celebrating the Whitbread Award, as well as the sponsored events. This was displayed in all the libraries in Humberside, and distributed to other libraries throughout the country. It achieved a meeting of the private and public sectors, and celebrated good literature whilst providing an opportunity for some talented graphic artists. There must be lots of "unlocked" opportunities like this, if we only had the time and energy to discover them.

An even more ambitious sponsorship opportunity arose in 1991, when we arranged with Rotherham Libraries to hire their brand new mobile library for two months in order to put our GCSE collection "on the road". This benefited us, because we did not wish to make a permanent investment in a mobile bookshop at that stage, and Rotherham, because they were temporarily unable to man the library—so instead of leaving it to stand idle, they were able to earn some money by putting it to effective use. We both achieved some significant publicity for our respective organisations, as well as promoting a very nice collection of books. (Though Rotherham did have to tangle with some bureaucratic red tape in the process!)

Finally, many a business enterprise is entitled to make a splash once in a while. We made ours in 1990, on the occasion of our 25th birthday. I had already been involved with the new West Yorkshire Playhouse in Leeds on some research into sponsorship for the theatre, and we decided that it would be an appropriate birthday celebration to sponsor one of its hospitality suites, if we could find a suitable play to interest our guests. Again, luck was on our side—one of the plays for the autumn season was a dramatisation of "Second from last in the Sack Race", by David Nobbs. The arrangements turned out to be quite complicated, and were made between us, and the Playhouse, and Mandarin, David Nobb's publishers. David Nobbs himself was very helpful, and although he was working on a film set for most of that day, he and his wife came to speak to our 25 guests after the performance. (Note: when you organise an event on premises that are not your own, you have to make even more certain that you have got everything—book displays, publicity material, etc.—right, because there is every little opportunity to rectify mistakes. When arranging events at theatres, it is also necessary to make sure all your guests know the exact arrangements, that they will arrive in the right place before the curtain goes up, and that they know where to go during the interval and for the reception afterwards.)

As I have indicated, working on author promotions is hard work, and can be nerve-wracking, but it is an extremely worthwhile occupation, and exciting, particularly when the burden is shared with other organisations. I think such sharing is particularly valuable to us today, when we are all—librarians, library suppliers and even publishers—much more stretched for resources than we used to be. Apart from this rather prosaic consideration, to co-operate is plain good sense.

Undoubtedly it makes for greater creative synergy. In each of our fields, we have some very talented people, and our talents are more likely to be fully exploited if we pool them in a "cross-disciplinary" approach to promotion.

Book fairs are simpler animals than fully-fledged author promotions, though they are also hard work. Most library suppliers will support librarians wishing to hold book fairs by attending them with a fairly extensive selection of stock. Librarians can help greatly by being as specific as possible about the types of book that they wish to be represented. Do they want books on certain topics? Fiction or non-fiction? Paperback or hardback? What age groups are being catered for?

Should some adult material be included? Will multiple copies be required? Is there a "price barrier" at which potential buyers are likely to become price sensitive? How many people are expected to attend the fair? What arrangements can be made to display the books/store spares? How much of his own equipment should the supplier bring with him? Should he bring publishers' posters and other publicity material? Will the catalogues produced by his own company be welcomed or not?

Book fairs are a potential way in to author promotions for librarians who have yet to try them, as a kind of "toe in the water" exercise. Some of the larger publishers are now expressing an interest in having author promotions in libraries, but the main fear they express is that of not being able to guarantee attendance from enough members of the public at any one time. Arranging an event at a book fair (particularly one featuring children's books if the author were a children's author) would reduce the likelihood of this. Publishers are now also becoming more aware that librarians, as well as library suppliers, find promotional kits, dumpbins and posters useful, though most still seem to expect librarians to acquire these through library suppliers, rather than asking for them directly.

Book fairs, and other gatherings where there is likely to be a high concentration of librarians and teachers—for example, seminars and training days—also present opportunities of venue when librarians wish library suppliers to contribute to their staff training or simply staff awareness of current trends and problems by giving papers on topical issues—for example, "The Potential Demise of the Schools Library Service", or "The Future of the Net Book Agreement". Not every library supplier employee who comes to a book fair will be happy to fufil this function, but most library suppliers have at least one potential speaker in their midst, who will be happy to contribute if he is given sufficient warning. (In spite of my initial comments about our tradesmanlike neutrality, we are not all dumb!)

I began this paper by saying that the publishers were the big fish in our pool. Perhaps rather unfairly, I also hinted that they were not always as interested in the rest of us (librarians, booksellers, library suppliers) as they might be. It is true that there has consistently been a gulf between librarians and publishers, and one which is only partially bridged by the activities and the good offices of the library supplier.

In order to expend our (diminishing in numbers) selves as efficiently and effectively as possible in the future, we need to try to close this gulf. Most publishers are themselves aware of it, but don't quite know what to do to remedy it. Sharing technologically-generated data may offer part of the solution, and several august bodies are already working on this. But the problem also needs tackling at grass roots level, by our attempting to address the challenges which confront us imaginatively and without prejudice. It is easy to rail against the "whale" publishers who are too preoccupied with their grandiose projects to take notice of us; but publishing houses are made up of individuals, and I have rarely met anyone from publishing who, on a one-to-one basis, was not sensitive and concerned. Librarians need to find ways of tapping in more to what publishers have to offer them in the way of expertise and wisdom gained at the coal face. I am aware that library suppliers have a pivotal role to play in this future dialogue. The best advice I can offer at the moment is: Use your library supplier to gain you the ear of the publisher to tell him what you need; and make it clear that this will not necessarily be a one-way service—that you will support him with your ideas, too.

Whales do not grow fat unless they are well-nourished on plenty of little fish—and they are intelligent creatures!

Linda Bennett is a director of H. & A. John (Booksellers) Ltd., part of the Woodfield & Stanley Group, and a Senior Lecturer in Management at the University of Huddersfield.

Copyright Linda Bennett, April 1993

# PART III

# Practical Tips

# CHAPTER 7

**HOW TO DO IT—extracts from Birmingham Public Libraries 'Image Book'**

**Planning It**
WHEN PLANNING WHAT TO DO, Don't be afraid to prioritise!

Libraries offer free access to all, but if they are to be effective, they can't be all things to all people.

It's far better to do one appropriate event well, promote it properly, organise related book displays, attract a large audience, milk it thoroughly for publicity, finishing with an article on it for the Library Association Record and a committee report rather than to rush about doing umpteen little things that don't quite come off because you didn't have time and weren't quite sure why you did them in the first place.

Once you've got an idea for a project that furthers your aims, before embarking on any potentially costly or time consuming action it is important to prepare a written plan—we'll call it your PROMOTIONAL PLAN.

The benefits of doing this are:

You don't waste valuable staff time or resources.
You make sure your project is promoted to the right people.
You have a better chance of positively influencing the decision-makers who can approve funding.

**Your Promotional Plan**
1. SWOT—Stand back from your idea for a moment and consider its strengths and weaknesses (strategies and resources), as well as opportunities and threats to it (the environment and the competition).
2. WHAT EXACTLY ARE YOU TRYING TO ACHIEVE?—What are your aims?
3. WHO ARE YOU TRYING TO REACH?—Who is your target audience?
4. WHAT IS YOUR MESSAGE?—What benefits will your project offer your target audience?

5. HOW ARE YOU BEST GOING TO REACH YOUR TARGET GROUP?—What resources do you need?
6. WHAT WOULD MAKE YOU FEEL THAT YOU'VE ACHIEVED YOUR OBJECTIVES?
7. CAN YOU THINK OF ANY OBJECTIVE WAYS OF MEASURING SUCCESS?—Realistic quantitative or quantitative goals.

Once you've prepared your plan and convinced the decision-makers of its value, you may find that resources aren't available so you may need to modify or abandon it.

"Someone's offered to do a free writing workshop for us next month. We'll probably stick a few posters up in the library for it. I hope not too many people come or we won't have space for them, mind you I don't think they will—I don't think people round here are interested much."

"We want to develop more active connections with our users. We aim to reach local people who are writing privately but lack confidence. We're saying that the library is the natural home of local writing. We'll need to target writers groups locally, get a mention in People to People, talk to users we know are keen. A one-off event with an author and discussion after about where to go next might be a good start; it might attract people who wouldn't dare to come to a writing group straight off. It wouldn't matter if only a few came, as long as they became the nucleus for a group. So if a group forms that would count as success."

... SO HOW MUCH WILL IT COST?!?!?!?!

Good Ideas tend to be flexible.

They can be done on a shoestring or developed into mega projects costing megabucks.

You need to decide what level your idea will work best at—and of course work out how much cash you could possible get your hands on!

START by working out your BOTTOM LINE.

What resources must you have for this project to happen effectively at all.

THEN think about what would be gained from additional resources.

"Well, we could do a workshop for local kids by phoning up the Head Teacher and doing a session using our own staff."

"Yes, but a nice poster about it would attract others and tell all our users that we do work with children. And they've met us before—if we could hire a professional to run it the kids would get far more from the experience."

"If it was a big name we could use it as an opportunity to promote our refurbished children's area."

'If it was a famous writer we could do it as part of Readers & Writers ... "

The main thing is to maximise resources, that means making sure we don't waste opportunities to develop good ideas further as well as ensuring that money isn't poured into ideas which won't gain from extra expense.

ONCE YOU HAVE PREPARED A PROMOTIONAL PLAN TALK TO YOUR LINE MANAGER in order to get the idea into the planning cycle and identify sources of funding. A resources checklist is included in part 3 to help you.

There are various possibilities for funding:

## The Promotions Budget
The allocation of the Promotions Budget is available in some systems. If you want to do a particular activity then it's put into your forward plan explaining how it fits into the department's strategy. This process should ensure that targeted activities are evenly spread in a large system, that there is no unnecessary duplication, and that where there is duplication resources are shared.

## Outside Funding
A project you are planning might be suitable for a grant from an outside body or an application to the Government's Inner City Partnership Programme (ICPP) so talk to your line manager and/or any 'specialists' who might be able to help.

The Regional Arts Board might be able to fund your project.

## Sponsorship
If you want to approach bigger companies, a co-ordinated approach is often the best option. In larger systems one member of staff may be given this remit. Do keep them informed of your intentions and use any expertise available.

You may wish to approach local shops and keep a look ou for other pockets of funding which might crop up.

## The Nitty Gritty
So, you've got your aims and objectives for the year ahead. These suggest a projec which you think will further them. You've included it in your forward plan and prepared a PROMOTIONAL PLAN.

You've secured funding for the project, NOW:

1. Work out what needs to be done when and who is going to do it. Decide wha advice and outside skills you'll need and plan how to get them.
2. Think through who else you ought to inform or involve. Estimate how muc time it will take and in what sorts of chunks, i.e. does anyone need to plan tim for concerted work on the project? Don't forget the safety angle, especially wit Children's Activities—see section *Children's Activities*.
3. Now it's time to consider how best to promote it.

## Promoting It

Promotion (or Public Relations as it is more usually called) is really about two-way communications, enabling:

Our chosen target group to know more about us.
Us to find out more about our target group's needs.

### Think about who you are trying to reach

You should know who your target group is, but which segments of that group do you wish to reach? For example, your promotion may be aimed at parents or carers of children under 5 but are you specifically interested in reaching parents/carers ...

From a particular area?
From a particular socio-economic group?
From a particular ethnic group or community?
Who use libraries already?
Who don't use libraries?

### Ask yourself what you want the promotion of your activity to achieve.
GET BUMS ON SEATS?
CONVEY A MESSAGE TO A SPECIFIC GROUP?
CONVEY A MESSAGE TO THE COMMUNITY AT LARGE?

The answers to these questions will help to identify who your audience are and the best way to reach them.

### Ways to reach our audience
Include:

1. Paid-for advertising.
2. "Free" editorial.
3. Printed publicity.
4. Word of mouth.

### Paid-for advertising

Costs lots, but it might be appropriate if the activity generates an income, and sometimes (e.g. Library Theatre) it's needed to place our stuff alongside the "competitors".

Find out more about the publication ... who reads it? ... where is it distributed? ... will it reach your target group?

### "Free" Editorial

Not really free—there are hidden costs involved—but editorial is much cheaper and more convincing than paid-for advertising. It is possible to get free editorial in local or national, general or specialised media, and you can help by ...

Thinking about the publications and TV/radio programmes most likely to reach your target group.

Notifying any promotions unit about your activity as far in advance as possible. Most press coverage is good for libraries and library services because it heightens awareness and can influence key decision makers ... but it's not always very good at getting bums on seats ... and don't be too upset if they get your name wrong, give the wrong date and print the picture back to front!

**Printed Publicity**
Posters and leaflets, glossy ones or in-house publications look nice, brighten the place up and reassure staff that publicity is in hand ... but are the right people reading them? and are they really necessary?

You need to consider how you are going to distribute publicity so that it will reach your target group e.g.

—to community venues—shops, pubs, etc.
—council departments e.g. leisure centres, neighbourhood offices, schools, museums.
—directly to individuals who might be interested. A letter or flyer to named contacts can work well, but you need to 'weed' mailing lists regularly, it's expensive to post lots of letters to people who have moved or died!

This will help you to decide how many leaflets or posters you need, and whether your budget can fund their production.

Good standards of publicity are needed to reach the particular groups of people who should be benefiting from services. Poor publicity which is badly designed, or not very well produced implies that the service is as bad as the publicity. If your library/service employs trained graphic designers ... make use of their professionalism ... remember to let them know what you like or don't like about the final design. Constructive criticism is always welcome. Think about how your design brief could have been improved.

**Word of Mouth:**
The most effective way to reach your audience—who doesn't listen to a personal recommendation from a trusted friend?

For some community events it may be almost all you need. A quick ring of contacts will alert the dedicated following who are bound to turn out.

Remember though that word of mouth can also work against you!—and the most brilliantly conceived promotional campaign won't "sell" a poor service twice.

And there are other ways to get your message to your target groups such as launches.

If you are planning an official launch you may need to involve senior management staff or councillors. Prepare the invitations and guest list well in advance for the necessary approval.

But is your launch really necessary? A prestigious do can attract publicity and brownie points for Birmingham Library Services, but only if it's launching something that needs that kind of treatment.

"Honoured as I am as Lord Mayor to have been invited to launch the installation of this marvellous new kettle in your splendid staff lounge ... "

## Doing It

### Booking It!

When you book someone to do a session for you, whether you're paying a fee or they're doing something on a voluntary basis, always write them a letter of confirmation with a clear outline of what you believe you have agreed. This is your chance to clarify in advance all those little details which might otherwise cause problems later, and although it's not a formal contract, you have something to refer to later if difficulties arise.

For instance:-

Dear (Upfront Theatre Company)

I'm writing to confirm that you will be (performing your play 'Revenge of the Killer Librarians' at Brum Heath Library, 34 Chamberlain Avenue, Brum Heath B94) on (May 5th) from (6.30–8.30pm) for a fee of (£35 plus your bus fares from the City Centre).

You will need to arrive at 5.00pm to set up. There is ample car parking space at the back of the Library, down the alley to the left of Safeways. Please ask for me on arrival and I'll show you where to change.

We will be publicising the event through posters in the library and local community, but as we agreed on the phone, you will undertake to contact local schools; we haven't had many performances of this kind before and I'm not sure that our normal publicity channels alone can guarantee a large audience.

It's a shame that the fire-breathing scene will have to be cut, but I'm sure you'll appreciate our concern for the children's safety.

As our budgets are very limited we can't offer to buy you a meal after the show, but there is a very reasonably priced cafe round the corner you might like to try.

If you bring an invoice for your fee plus expenses on the night we will pass it for payment immediately. We're told that it currently takes about one month for cheques to be sent out once the invoice has arrived.

We're all very much looking forward to your performance. If you're happy with the arrangements outlined above, please sign one copy of this letter and return it to the address above. If you have any queries, don't hesitate to contact me.

Yours sincerely,

C. J. Overleaf, Community Librarian

### Tickets

It may be a good idea to issue tickets for events even if they are free. Don't hand them out to all but publicise that they're available from the desk.

If people have proper tickets then they're more likely to turn up—who wants to waste a freebie? And it will help you to gain an idea of numbers.

Experience suggests that you can allow for about 1/3 of those with tickets actually turning up to the event.

You can also send 'complimentary' tickets to sponsors, press, politicians etc. But remember that there will be a cost implication for tickets so you'll need to get funding approved.

**Timing**
Promotions need full details of an activity at least two months in advance for inclusion in events listings, monthly broadsheets etc., and so that press releases can be prepared and publicity can be ready at least one month before the event.

BUT with all the forward planning in the world, sometimes opportunities crop up AT THE LAST MINUTE which it seems a shame to miss.

"The Queen's on the phone asking if she can visit us next month!"

"Well, she's not in my forward plan ... "

Before you say yes to it, think:

Does it fit my aims and objectives?
Is it really now or never?
Is it practical in the time?
Can funding be identified for it?

"Well, she doesn't want a fee and we are targeting elderly women ..."

If you're sure it's worth it then go for it!

We'll do our best to support you.

DON'T PANIC—plan what time you do have, think about useful shortcuts—the quickest way to alert your target audience. Tell everyone who needs to know as soon as possible.

Have you invited everyone you want to come?

Do you have enough people available to cope with emergencies?

Do you have enough chairs/cups/tables?

Is the place safe? Watch out for loose electrical leads, wobbly scenery etc.

Have you sorted out changing rooms for performers?

Are you expecting the press and if so are you prepared for them?

Are toilets signposted?

Will people need somewhere to leave coats/wet umbrellas/pushchairs etc?

What do you need to provide to ensure access to the disabled?

Can you do anything to improve the appearance of the library?

Introduce the event.

Tell people how long it lasts.

Explain any details about refreshments, toilets etc.

Plug any other events/activities your audience might be interested in.
Provide opportunities for people to give feedback on the event.

How did they hear about it?

Did they enjoy it?

Was it what they expected?

Provide a comments book and ask staff to listen out for comments and jot them down. Count how many attended.

## Afterwards
It's all over—

Clear up, throw away out of date publicity and congratulate yourselves on having made it through the experience.

Now is the time to decide if it 'worked'.

Go back to your original plans and ask:

Did it achieve your aims?
If not, do you know why not?
Did it achieve any other aims you hadn't expected?
What anecdotal evidence do you have to show how successful it was?
What objective evidence do you have to show how successful it was?
—see the tips on Monitoring and evaluation in the appendix for ideas.

Who should you tell about it?

Line managers, specialists, outside agencies, other departments interested in running the same event. Is it worth writing up for the LAR or letting other people in BLS know about it?

Do you want advice on how to improve it next time, if so who from?

AND DON'T FORGET—WE ALL MAKE MISTAKES.

This book is written by people who have scribbled scrappy notices and held events with no publicity, audience or artist merit in their time.

But be honest—it's much more useful to analyse what went wrong and share bad experiences as well as good than to pretend it went brilliantly.

And don't overlook positive gains such as the staff working well as a team, developing new skills, confidence and ideas ... and enjoying themselves!

**Monitoring and Evaluating your Project**

Some basic questions you should be asking before and after:

1. DID IT HAPPEN?
   - if so, how?
   - if not, why not?
   - what problems occurred?
2. TOTAL COST OF ACTIVITY?
   - money for publicity, hire, etc.
   - staff time utilised
3. HOW MANY PEOPLE ATTENDED RESPONDED?
   - what was the cost per person benefiting?
   - how many people benefited by sectors of population (age, sex, race etc?)
4. WHAT WAS MY TARGET GROUP? (specific)
   - what proportion of target group benefited?
   i.e. how great was the impact?
   - did the target group make more use than other groups?
   - cost per event per (target) capita.
5. WHAT HAVE I LEARNED FROM THE EVENT?
   - method of organisation
   - detail of what took place
   - linkages/networks created with others
   - other areas

While it is important to pre-plan with regard to promotion etc, it is important also to allocate time for monitoring and evaluation. This should not simply be an optional extra!

Remember to be clear about what the projects aims are. There is a need to be precise also. It is not enough to simply say that the aim was to "improve the library's image".

**Planning an event involving children and carers**

Many of the factors involved in planning any event in the library are equally applicable to events involving children. The issue of the safety of individuals in the library is always important but this takes on a greater significance where children are involved. These are some of the things to consider when planning an event for children.

How many children can you safely cope with in your particular library? Would it be appropriate to make the event ticket only?

Have outside visitors been recommended to you, not only for the quality of the performance but also for their suitability and desirability to work with young children? Are they offering a different experience to children than we ourselves can offer?

Is the environment safe? Is the equipment out of reach and all trailing wires taped down? Is the activity in itself safe? Are outside presenters covered by insurance if their activity is potentially dangerous?

Is the staffing level adequate? Is there a member of staff who can keep an eye on the door to ensure young children to not leave the library before their parents arrive to collect them, or who can take children to the toilet if necessary?

If library staff are going to present the session, are they well trained and given adequate time to be prepared? Are less experienced staff given the support they need?

Are you prepared for all eventualities? Have you prepared an extra activity in case your planned activity finishes early, or a visitor is late, or a press photographer delays the start of the session?

If the press arrive to take a photograph always ask to see their press pass to check their credentials, particularly as they are photographing children. A child should never be allowed outside.